C000271505

CHILE

Compact Guide: Chile is the ultimate quick-reference guide to this incredibly varied country. It tells you everything you need to know about Chile's attractions, from the bustle of downtown Santiago to the remote fjords of Patagonia and from the deserts of the Atacama to the lakes and volcanoes of the Central Valley.

This is one of 133 Compact Guides, combining the interests and enthusiasms of two of the world's best-known information providers: Insight Guides, whose titles have set the standard for visual travel guides since 1970, and Discovery Channel, the world's premier source of nonfiction television programming.

APA PUBLICATIONS

Part of the Langenscheidt Publishing Group

Star Attractions

An instant reference to some of Chile's most popular tourist attractions to help you to set your priorities.

Santiago p22

The Andes p29

Viña del Mar p34

Atacama Desert p38

El Tatio geysers p50

Lago Villarrica p62

Lago Todos Los Santos p65

Chiloé churches p66

Torres del Paine p73

Temuco Market p61

Easter Island p76

Introduction

Places

Culture

Leisure

Practical Information

Chile – Island on the Continent

Opposite: riding out in the Elqui Valley

'Chile is God's mechanism for keeping Argentina from the Pacific'…'Chileans always have to lie down lengthwise to avoid getting wet feet'. Such jokes are inevitable considering the dimensions of this South American land. If you take a quick glance at a world map, you hardly notice Chile, so narrow is this country caught between the Andes and the Pacific. Yet what it lacks in width it makes up for in length: the world's longest country contains some of the most dramatic and varied scenery on earth, from snow-capped mountains to deep fjords, pluming volcanoes to blooming deserts and dense forests to crystal lakes. From the desert extremes of the north to the Mediterranean climes of the center to the raw isolation of the south, Chile's weather chops and changes with its scenery. Landscape and climate forge a people and, while it has been said that everyone here is more European than in Europe, there are worlds between the hardy folk of Patagonia and the sophisticated inhabitants of Santiago.

Indigenous crafts

5

'Such a country should be called an island,' wrote the Chilean geographer Benjamin Subercaseaux, and Chile has certainly often gone its own way. Its founder, Pedro de Valdivia, was not in search of gold but of land, and was the only Spanish conqueror of the New World to bring a wife, who steadfastly stood by his side. In 1541 he established the ground plan of Santiago, in the fertile Mapocho Valley, and as early as 1567 Chile already had its own justice system while the rest of the continent had to rely on Lima in Peru. Despite having fertile land and a largely temperate climate, however, the Chilean population remained stubbornly low. It was only in the second half of the 19th century that a wave of European immigrants began to arrive. But unlike the other South American countries, where the Spanish were predominant, Chile attracted farmers from Switzerland and Germany; gold miners from Serbia and Croatia; and sheep farmers and tradesmen from England and Wales.

Central Valley vernacular

Today's Chile remains distinctive for its ethnic mix, and the country's inventiveness and flexibility have brought it considerable economic success, earning it the epithet 'the Latin American country that works'.

Position and landscape

Bounded in the north by Peru and Bolivia, on its long eastern border by Argentina, and to the west by the Pacific Ocean, Chile was affectionately dubbed 'the thin country' by the Nobel prize-winning Chilean poet Pablo Neruda. It extends about 4,300km (2,700 miles) from its boundary

The High Andes

with Peru in the tropical zone (latitude 17.30°S), to the tip of South America at Cape Horn (latitude 56°S), with an average width of just over 160km (100 miles). Continental Chile and its offshore islands comprise 736,903 sq km (284,520 sq miles), making it the fourth smallest country in South America; but added to this, Chile lays claim to a vast Antarctic territory, and exercises sovereignty over Easter Island, the Juan Fernández Archipelago and the volcanic islets of Sala y Gómez, San Félix and San Ambrosio in the South Pacific.

Chile's landscape is chiefly mountainous, with the Andes dominating and reaching elevations (along the northern part of the eastern border with Argentina) of nearly 7,000m (23,000ft). This topography is primarily the result of forces that have been at work for millions of years; large subterranean blocks, known as the Nazca and Antarctic plates, are thought to have gradually moved across from the Pacific and worked their way under the American plate, lifting the earth's crust and causing earthquakes and volcanic eruptions as well as numerous continental changes. And these geological shifts are by no means over: Easter Island, on the Nazca plate, is moving toward Chile at the rate of around 1m (3ft) every year.

Around 100 million years ago there was only one cordillera, or mountain range, running parallel to the coast. As a result of the pressure from the plates below, this range grew until it eventually turned into an enormous massif. When this collapsed back into itself, roughly along the line of its highest ridge, the large peaks and troughs we know today were formed: the High Andes, the coastal range, and the long, fertile valley between the two. South of Puerto Montt, powerful glaciation in the Andes was followed by extreme erosion, so that the cordilleras were flattened more here than in the north. As the sea levels rose globally after the last Ice Age, the waters of the Pacific moved far inside the ice-gouged valleys of Patagonia and the Chiloé archipelago, with their fjord-like landscapes. Lakes formed in the melt basins of glaciers. Intensive volcanic activity, in central Chile especially, resulted in the formation of several unusual natural phenomena, including geysers, cone-shaped mountains and thermal springs.

The north of Chile is almost synonymous with dryness. With the exception of the odd oasis, El Norte Grande (The Great North, between the Peruvian border and Antofagasta 720km/450 miles farther south) is uninhabitable desert. In fact, because of the Humboldt Current, a cold ocean current flowing north along the coast of Chile, and an area of high pressure above the Pacific, this is the driest zone in the entire world. It is, however, also enormously rich in minerals: Chile is the world's largest producer of copper, and the largest supplier of molybdenum and lithium.

Geysers at El Tatio (above) and the arid Atacama

The high and barren Andes along its eastern edge are broken up by snow-covered volcanoes, many of them extinct or dormant, but always fascinating in their majesty. A whole range of browns, beiges, grays and rusty-reds captivate the beholder, even in The Small North, El Norte Chico (500km/310 miles north of Valparaíso), and especially in the bizarre salt landscapes. Between 80 and 160mm (3–6 in) of rain fall every seven to 10 years between Copiapó and La Serena, creating magnificent carpets of flowers in the lonely desert landscape. Hordes of visitors arrive at these times to admire them.

The relentless Pacific

7

The Mediterranean climate of central Chile (latitude 30–40°S) creates a pleasant atmosphere in which to live. In the northern part of this zone – where the meadows and fields are filled with weeping willows and poplar trees, fields of sunflowers add a dash of powerful color to the landscape, and the mountains turn beautifully purple in the evenings – the flat terracotta roofs of the old country houses can be glimpsed among the greenery surrounding them. This is where Chile's internationally reputed wine is produced, where delicious fruit grows, and where agriculture is at its most intensive and successful – and Santiago lies at its cultural and economic heart. In the southern half of the central valley the snow-covered volcanoes, many of them active as opposed to the ones further north, stand out sharply against the mountain range behind them. Their perfect conical shapes reflect on the quiet waters in the Lake District providing some of the most splendid scenery in temperate South America, complete with vast expanses of magnificent forest and lush valleys used largely for dairy farming.

Volcano country

The south – made up of Patagonia and Tierra del Fuego – gets little snow, but a great deal of rain. The countless square kilometers of fjord landscape are almost incomparably rich in marine life, and salmon farming is widespread in the south of the country. Chile is the second-largest salmon exporter in the world after Norway. On a trip through northern Patagonia along a road masterfully hewn out of the landscape, the Carretera Austral, the fjords, forests, glaciers and pampas can all be seen to best advantage. In southern Patagonia the Cordillera del Paine – with its steep rock faces and peaks bordering the foothills of the Southern Ice Field to the northwest and the pampas to the east – is most impressive.

The northern part of Tierra del Fuego is marvelously desolate, conjuring up images of the original inhabitants sitting huddled around smoking campfires *(see page 74)*. The mountainous southern part with its forests is easily accessible only on the Argentinian side.

Climate and when to go

The climate in the coastal regions of the hot north and of central Chile is actually cooler than you'd expect. The cold Humboldt Current is the main cause of this, carrying Antarctic waters northwards along the coast and mixing them with equally cold waters from the depths of the Peruvian Trench. They cool the air masses from below, and a great deal of fog is formed as a result. The sun often only manages to clear the mist by the early afternoon, so mornings are cool even in summer and temperatures seldom exceed 25°C (80°F) in the afternoon.

The proximity of the Andes and the resulting cold mountain winds are the main reason for the sharp drop in temperatures in the foothill region. Though daytime temperatures in Santiago often exceed 30°C (88°F) during January and February, they drop to 12–15°C (55–60°F) at night. The same applies to the lake region in central Chile. In Punta Arenas the daytime temperature in sunny weather reaches 20°C (80°F) and drops to around 5°C (40°F) at night. That's combined with a west wind that often whistles across the landscape at around 80kmph (50mph), making the mighty treetops sway visibly.

Chile's location in the southern hemisphere means that the seasons here are the opposite of Europe and the USA. Winter here is from May through September, and an ideal time to go skiing. November through March, and the hottest months of January and February, are a good period for vacations at the resorts, lakes, fjords and glaciers. The Chileans are fond of taking vacations in their own country during the summer months, so it's always a good idea to book peak-period vacations well in advance.

Flora and fauna

There are around 95 protected national parks in Chile, all of them administered by CONAF (National Forestry Corporation). It maintains a series of bases where travelers

8

Coastal contrasts

can receive information and assistance. Hunting and camping out in the open (because of the danger of fire) are prohibited in these regions, but there are usually good hotels and campsites to make up for that.

The flora and fauna of Chile are every bit as varied as its geography and climate. In the north, cacti and scrubland draw all the moisture they need from the coastal fog *(camanchaca)*. The cacti around here reach heights of 3.4m (11ft). In the arid highlands, reed-like cushion plants and high-moor bog vegetation *(bofedales)* grow close to rivers or lakes and provide food for the different species of cameloids found in South America. The emerald-green lakes are home to coot, geese, ducks and flamingos, while condors fly high in the mountains. Mountain-dwellers such as the chinchilla, vizcacha and opossum are hardly anywhere to be found. The magnificent Parque Nacional Lauca *(see page 40–1)*, at 4,000m (13,200ft), contains an impressive cross-section of this flora and fauna.

The variety of Chilean forest is at its most evident in the rainiest regions. Elsewhere, the Chilean palm *(Jubaea chilensis)*, whose marrow is used to make a honey-like juice *(miel de palma),* grows in the region around Santiago, but has unfortunately almost died out. From the coastal mountains south of Concepción to the east of Temuco, there are also some highly impressive monkey-puzzle trees *(Araucaria araucana)*, which are the emblem of the national parks.

These enormous ancient trees can reach heights of 50m (165ft) and have triangular leaves shaped like scales. Their fruit can grow to the size of a child's head, and their finger-length seeds (roasted) have been a favorite food with the Amerindians since time immemorial. In the forests of southern Chile there are various species of Southern beech *(Nothofagus)*, including the widespread *Coigüe*,

Desert dwellers

In the forest

which doesn't shed its leaves, but uses them to save water for the dry season.

In winter the red bell-shaped flowers of the copihue *(Lapageria rosea)* appear; it's the Chilean national plant, and can be seen wrapped around tree trunks in the forests. Around Puerto Montt and on Chiloé there are some magnificent ancient specimens of Fitzroy cypress *(Fitzroya cupressoides)*, a species that can attain an age of 4,000 years. Today the trees are protected, because their wood has been over-forested as it is highly valued for its strength as a building material.

The copihue

Chile is home to 76 species of lizard, 25 of octopus and squid, and six of snake. In the far north, the Andean rabbit pops its head out from behind rocks. In the central region rabbits, hares, mice, wildcats and the Chilean beaver scamper round forests. And throughout Chile there are nine species of penguin.

Though you will hardly ever see the puma for which Chile is famed, you will certainly spot numerous cameloids. The llama *(Lama guanicoe glama)* is the largest of the four members of the camel family in South America, and was reared as a pack animal by the Indians. It produces around 4kg (9lb) of thick wool annually. The animal knows its limits as far as exertion is concerned: it will carry weights of up to 40kg (75lb) over a distance of 25km (15 miles) a day, but if more is added it simply lies down.

The smaller alpaca *(Lama guanicoe pacos)* has so much soft wool that it can hardly see where it's going. The even smaller, fine-limbed guanaco *(Lama guanicoe)* lives wild, mainly in Patagonia, and is a protected species. The graceful vicuña *(Lama vicugna)*, the smallest of the cameloids, also lives wild; its wool (around 180g/6oz every two years) is so silky and fine that its quality is surpassed only by silk. In 1973 all that were left were around

Alpaca herd

1,000 vicuñas, and only drastic protection of the species allowed their numbers to increase to 32,000 by 2002.

To help you differentiate between the various cameloids, llamas vary from black and brown to white; alpacas are various shades of brown; and vicuñas and guanacos are an elegant shade of beige.

Administration

Chile is a presidential republic. The president is elected directly by the people for a term of six years, and for that he needs an absolute majority. The National Congress consists of the House of Representatives with 120 members and the Senate with 38 senators elected and nine appointed for eight-year terms. The ex-presidents of the republic become lifetime senators.

The Republic of Chile is divided into 12 administrative regions designated by Roman numerals (running from north to south) and Santiago and its surroundings, known as the Región Metropolitana.

Parliament building in Valparaíso

Economy

Chile is a free-market economy and between the mid-1980s and the mid-1990s, the majority of state enterprises, including the main public utilities were privatized, leaving Codelco, a copper producer, and the Enap oil company as the only large enterprises that continue to be state-owned.

With a small domestic market, the economy is driven by exports and, as for centuries, the country's wealth is derived mainly from its natural resources. In the past, nitrates and silver were important; today, copper, wood pulp, farmed salmon and fresh fruit (50 percent of it grapes) predominate, and are exported to markets around the world, led by the United States, Japan and China.

Since democracy was restored in 1990, Chile has become increasingly integrated with the rest of the world and, in economic terms, this is reflected in its growing network of free-trade agreements, which includes the European Union, the United States, Canada, Mexico and South Korea. In addition, in early 2005, it initiated free-trade negotiations with China – a key destination for the country's copper and forestry exports – and started exploratory talks with Japan.

For a long time now the national economy has been supported by a broad middle class, and positive economic development since the mid-1980s has turned Chile into the 'tiger state' of Latin America. It almost always attains the highest growth rates on the subcontinent and, in 2004, the economy expanded by 6.1 percent. Inflation has been controlled and fiscal discipline has become one of Chile's economic hallmarks, although taxes are somewhat higher

11

Saltpeter transport and the copper mine at Chuquicamata

Downtown Santiago

than in other Latin American countries and value added tax alone is 19 percent.

Alongside the classic sectors of mining and agriculture, tourism is playing an increasingly important role in the national revenue. Some 1.8 million overseas tourists now visit Chile annually and, although many are from neighboring countries, an increasing number of visitors are from Europe, North America and, most recently, Asia.

Political developments

Inaugurated in 1821, Chile has had a long history of representative democracy, with only a few short-lived exceptions, of which the Pinochet dictatorship (1973–90) is the most notable.

Progressive democratic development – in Latin American terms at least – is certainly what defined Chile at the beginning of the 20th century. The country's victory in the War of the Pacific (1879–1883) had won it territories in the north with great mineral resources. Increasing prosperity necessitated a change in Chilean society, and a bourgeois middle class began to develop in the towns as jobs became more plentiful in the administration and service sectors.

President Arturo Alessandri, elected in 1920 and in power until 1924, introduced social reforms; these included a right to work, and gave Chile a leading role in South America. During his second term of office (1932–38) the Partido Socialista de Chile was formed by the miners' and workers' associations. The coalition of socialists, communists and the radical left wing of the party, known as the Frente Popular, voted in the first People's Front government in 1938. Until 1952 a succession of these governments contributed to an improvement in living conditions for the lower classes. Energy production and raw material extraction were stepped up considerably, and industrialization took pride of place. In 1953 the most powerful trade union in today's Chile was founded: the Central Unitaria de Trabajadores (CUT).

Jorge Alessandri, the president from 1958 to 1964, succeeded in implementing the construction of social housing and in stemming inflation, which had gone out of control as a result of corruption, administrative inefficiency and party dishonesty.

In 1964 Eduardo Frei Montalva was elected as candidate for the Partido Demócrata Cristiano (PDC). His Revolution in Freedom program aimed to restructure society and nationalize the country's copper mines, which accounted for 80 percent of exports. He tried very hard to improve social amenities (such as housing and childcare) and education. But his attempts at agricultural and industrial reforms were less successful: he achieved no

Eduardo Frei Montalva

consensus in a country that at that time was considered a paragon of democracy.

In 1970, Marxist physician Salvador Allende (uncle of the award-winning novelist Isabel Allende, *see page 82*) gained a small majority of 36.9 percent for his party Unidad Popular (UP), an association of communists, socialists and left-wing splinter groups, in the name of 'the Chilean way of Socialism'. He won parliamentary support with the help of the Christian Democrats (PDC), stepping up agricultural reform (with expropriations) and nationalizing copper production as well as several other branches of industry.

He faced trouble in 1971, however, when some groups emphasized their call for a follow-up on election promises and occupied several industrial and agricultural enterprises; 30,000 rich Chileans promptly left the country, supply bottlenecks and strikes increased, and investment ground to a halt. Conservatives and the right-dominated Supreme Court saw their opportunity to grab power and put pressure on the army. On September 11 1973 the far-right leaning armed forces, with the tacit support of the US, assumed power in a putsch, and Allende committed suicide during an assault on the presidential palace.

A brutal junta, formed by the supreme commanders of the military and the police under General Augusto Pinochet, dissolved parliament and declared a "state of emergency" (this lasted until 1978, and also from 1984 to 1988). Political parties and trade unions were prohibited, the constitution (including all civil rights) was repealed, and freedom of the press was severely curtailed. Many former government supporters fled abroad. The military's violent treatment of members of the opposition led – after a protest by Chilean bishops about human rights violations – to UN resolutions in 1974 and again in 1975, 1978 and 1983 calling for an end to torture and for the release of all political prisoners.

The military takes over

Allende and followers

The early years of the Pinochet dictatorship were characterized by a radical path towards a market economy, accompanied initially by a powerful recession and high unemployment. But from 1977 onwards Chile opened up to international trade, lowered trade tariffs and tried to interest outside investors. After a further recession in the early 1980s, the economic situation stabilized.

General Pinochet

A constitution passed in 1981 separated the office of president – which General Pinochet had occupied since 1974 – from the junta, and limited the term of office until 1989. In 1987, political parties were permitted once more, and in a referendum held in October 1988 the Chileans decided by a margin of 54.7 percent against a further eight-year term of office for Pinochet.

After presidential and parliamentary elections in December 1989, a center-left coalition under President Patricio Aylwin took over control, and marked Chile's return to democracy, although General Pinochet stayed on as army commander until 1998. The new government of the Concertación (de los Partidos por la Demócracia) regarded the reinforcement of democracy, the battle against poverty and a stable economic and monetary policy as its main tasks. Two further Concertación governments followed, headed by President Eduardo Frei Ruiz-Tagle (son of Eduardo Frei Montalva) and President Ricardo Lagos, whose term ends in March 2006, Under these two governments, notable progress has been achieved in the quality of public infrastructure and services as well as in reinforcing civil liberties and reducing poverty, although not in improving the country's very unequal income distribution.

In the early 1990s, a National Commission for Truth and Reconciliation was formed to investigate the deaths and disappearances that took place under the military government and in 2004, another commission investigated the use of torture by the dictatorship. In 1998, General Pinochet was arrested on human rights charges filed by a Spanish judge during a visit to London where he was held until March 2000. After his return to Chile, the local courts found the former dictator unfit to stand trial and, in 2004, he forfeited the loyalty of his dwindling supporters after it was revealed that he and his family held multi-million-dollar overseas bank accounts, containing funds allegedly taken from fiscal revenue.

Chile – country of wine

Wine-making has a long tradition

Chile's founder Pedro de Valdivia brought the first vines to the country, laying the foundations of an important industry. Every country estate in the old days had its own church and its own vineyards, where wine was grown for Mass. From 1851 onwards the wine industry grew to become an important part of the economy. New vines

and also wine experts were brought in from France. The Chileans consider themselves especially fortunate that their vines were not destroyed by the phylloxera beetle and similar pests, like the ones in Europe.

Chilean wine is to South America what French wine is to Europe. Most of the wine estates are open to visitors – not only the old vaulted basements, but also the manor houses and often their magnificent grounds too.

On the eastern edge of Santiago is the oldest vineyard in Chile, **Viña Cousiño Macul** (Avenida Quilín 7100, tours Monday to Friday 11am and 4pm, Saturday 11am; advance booking required, tel: 02-351 4175).

Maipo vineyards and harvest time

15

Dawnings of civilization: the first mummies

Cave paintings near Putre, in the Great North *(see page 40)*, document the first settlement in Chile 11,000 years ago. But life on the coast began with the Chinchorro culture in around 6000BC, who were the first people anywhere in the world to master the art of mummification.

They kept the secret of embalming their dead for 4,000 years: having removed all the internal organs, they dried the corpses with embers and then tied them to sticks and stood them up. The belly was filled with a mixture of earth, wool, feathers and plant fibers, while the muscles of arms and legs were replaced by layers of reeds, plant fibers and earth. Wigs were made from dead people's hair, and they painted the faces with white, red or black earth, and the bodies with colors made from iron oxide and manganese. Cloaks made from plant fibers 'warmed' the dead, who were buried lying flat on their backs.

Mummy at San Pedro

Today's people

The Chileans are a mixture of Europeans and American Indians. The *mestizos*, resulting from early interbreeding of Spaniards and Indians, blended in with immigrants

Friends on Chiloé Island

of many different origins: German, Swiss, French, Italian, English, Serbian and Croatian.

But today's population displays a strong sense of cultural identity, which can be traced to the predominance of the Spanish language, the Roman Catholic religion and the comparative isolation of Chile from the rest of South America. The majority of Chileans are Catholic (70 percent), while 15 percent are Protestant. The Araucanian Indians (Mapuches, *see below*) form the only significant ethnic minority, with a religion that is a blend of ancient shamanistic beliefs and Roman Catholicism.

Of the country's 15.1 million inhabitants, 87 percent live in the cities (40 percent in Greater Santiago); the average population density in the country overall is 19.9 people per square kilometer, but in Patagonia there is just one person per square kilometer.

Virgen de la Inmaculada Concepción, Santiago

The Mapuches

You cannot travel anywhere in the deep south of Chile without noticing the influence of the country's original natives, who call themselves *Mapuches* ('people of the earth'). They lived in scattered settlements from the Aconcagua Valley in the north, as far south as the Island of Chiloé. They also inhabited most of what is now Argentine Patagonia. Numbering in the region of 500,000 today, the Mapuches speak their own language and maintain many of their centuries-old customs. The Mapuches had, and still have today, a relatively hierarchical society based on family structures.

Before the Inca incursion of the 15th century, this tribe dominated the 1,300km (780 mile)-long region west of the Andes between Illapel and Puerto Montt. Warlike and freedom-loving, they never bowed to the Spanish Crown. King Philip II complained that Chile 'cost him the blood of his nobility', for around 50,000 Spanish soldiers died in the battles with the Mapuche – compared with some 300 elsewhere in South America. They were subjugated as far as the Río Maule, but from there they made things continually difficult for the Spanish.

The Mapuche were polygamous, and led a nomadic existence with their herds, organizing themselves into family clans without any political or economic coherence. The family head *(cacique)* was chief simply in the respect that he was allowed the prestige of having up to 10 wives, and the families elected chieftains *(toqui)* only if war threatened. For food they cultivated corn, beans, squash, potatoes, chili peppers and other vegetables, and fished, hunted and kept guinea pigs for meat. They had llamas as pack animals and as a source of wool, and a man's wealth was reckoned in terms of the size of his llama herd.

Market day in Puerto Montt

After centuries of an unhappy co-existence with the descendants of the colonial invaders, at the end of the 19th century the Chilean state resettled the Mapuches on to reservations south of the Bío-Bío River. Each clan was granted land, amounting to around 300,000 hectares (750,000 acres) in total, which was not for sale to white people. Today Mapuches in the south continue to live in traditional communities and their straw-thatched round, oval or square wooden houses *(ruca)* can be seen around Temuco, Osorno, Villarrica and Pucón. Families live off the land and scratch a living from handicrafts made from silver, wool and *coirón* (a straw-like material used for baskets). This tough rural farming life no longer attracts many of the young, though, and they leave in droves for the cities. Many have migrated to Santiago forming tight-knit communities, keeping traditional customs alive.

17

Weaving for a living

The spirit of the Mapuches is by no means dimmed, however. Many hang on to age-old beliefs in the lord of the earth, Ngenechen, who unites the essence of man and woman, youth and old age, and controls a panoply of deities. The shamans, or *machi*, are in contact with them and summon them in a trance during rituals to awaken the fertility of the earth. The dances on such occasions are accompanied by drums, trumpets and pipes.

On important occasions the women wear silver jewelry which is believed to absorb positive and dispel negative energies; a silver headband makes thoughts wiser, while chest decorations protect the heart from the evil of others. The women never cut their hair because steady growth is equivalent to a never-ending process of becoming. And so the Mapuches' traditions live on, fueled by the belief in a perfect balance between positive and negative forces, and good and evil and Ngenechen, the force of life, creation and love.

Historical Highlights

Around 12,000BC After the Ice Age tribes from the north wander into the region occupied by today's Chile. As hunters and gatherers, they settle in the oases along the rivers and coasts.

Around 6,000BC The Chinchorro are the first people in the world to mummify their dead, in the region around Arica.

3rd–11th century AD The north is strongly influenced by the Tiwakanu culture, based around Lake Titicaca. The Mapuches arrive in Chile via the Argentine Pampas, and rule the region from Illapel to Puerto Montt.

1470 The Incas invade Chile and are halted by the warlike Mapuches at the Río Maule. They subjugate themselves to the tribes of northern Chile. Inca rule ends when the country is conquered by the Spanish.

1494 The Treaty of Tordesillas divides the Americas between the Spanish and Portuguese, granting all territory west of Brazil to Spain.

1520 Fernão de Magalhães (Magellan), a Portuguese in the service of the Spanish Crown, is the first to sail through the straits in Patagonia that were later named for him.

1535 Diego de Almagro marches southward from Cusco through the Andes. But cold, hunger and altitude sickness force him to turn back when he reaches Copiapó.

1540 Pedro de Valdivia is assigned the task of conquering Chile by Spanish *conquistador* Francisco Pizarro. He successfully reaches the Río Mapocho, where he founds Santiago on February 12 1541. In 1553 he meets his death at the hands of the Mapuches; legend has it that he was tied to a tree and forced to swallow molten gold.

1557, 1558 The two Mapuche heroes Lautaro and Caupolicán are killed fighting the Spanish.

1562 End of the Spanish conquest of Chile.

1567 Santiago receives the Real Audiencia (supreme jurisdiction) for the colony of Chile.

1704 The Scottish-Spanish pirate Alexander Selkirk requests to be marooned on the Mas-a-Tierra (renamed Isla Robinson Crusoe in 1966), only to be rescued four years later. Daniel Defoe's novel *Robinson Crusoe* is based on his experiences.

1746 University of San Felipe and the Mint are built in Santiago.

1767 Spanish King Carlos III has all Jesuits driven out of the colony.

1778 Chile receives a large amount of administrative freedom from the Spanish Crown.

1788–96 Ambrosio O'Higgins, born in Ireland, achieves a cease-fire with the Mapuches as governor of Chile; he also abolishes forced labor and introduces cotton, tobacco and rice cultivation. In 1796 his king makes him Viceroy of Peru.

September 18 1810 Appointment of Chile's first self-elected national government, a junta, in order to forestall French ownership claims in Hispano-America as a result of Napoleon's battles in Spain.

1811 The junta, led by the wealthy Santiago family, the Carreras, convokes the first National Congress on July 4.

1814 Bernardo O'Higgins, son of the former governor and a radical member of the junta, beats the royalists with a national army. After his defeat in Rancagua he flees to Argentina, and joins forces there with General San Martín, a sympathetic freedom fighter.

1817 O'Higgins and San Martín cross the Andes with 5,000 men, defeat the royalists at Chacabuco and enter Santiago in triumph.

February 12 1818 Chile declares its independence from Spanish rule, appointing O'Higgins as Director Supremo. In April, after more battles, Chile's independence is finally established at the Battle of Maipú.

1820s onwards Chile begins to mine its rich mineral deposits, creating new-found riches.

1823 O'Higgins resigns in the face of opposition from the clergy and the nobility. He dies in Peru in 1842, and his body is not returned to his homeland until 1869.

1828 The bicameral parliamentary system is introduced. The civil war between liberals and conservatives plunges the country into chaos. Diego Portales, minister from 1830 to 1832 and from 1835 onwards, drafts the constitution of 1933. He is respected as the creator of the republic, with many of his reforms forming the basis for Chile's present constitution.

1836–9 The government of José Tomás de Ovalle is bolstered by a successful war against the Peruvian-Bolivian Confederation.

1839 Chile prints its first banknotes.

1843 The University of Chile is founded.

1879–83 The War of the Pacific erupts with Peru and Bolivia. Victorious Chile gains the Great North with its mineral resources.

1886 José Manuel Balmaceda is elected president, and instigates a program of public building and social policies. Though a conservative uprising deposes him in 1890, and places Jorge Montt at the head of government, many of his policies are continued by his successors.

1888 Chile annexes Easter Island.

1989 The poet Gabriela Mistral, the only Latin American woman to have won the Nobel Prize for Literature, is born.

1904 Pablo Neruda, Chile's most successful poet, is born.

1920–24 President Arturo Alessandri introduces fundamental political and social reforms, but the army's opposition to his policies forces him to flee to Argentina.

1924–31 General Ibáñez del Campo takes over as president but, after a period of economic problems, he too is driven into exile in Argentina.

1938–52 People's Front governments (Frente Popular, a center-left coalition).

1941 Chile's most popular national park, Parque Nacional Puyehue, is opened to protect 65,000 hectares (152,500 acres) of forest land.

1964–70 The Christian Democrat Eduardo Frei Montalva is president, and undertakes a program of successful social reforms.

1970 The left-wing coalition Popular Unity, led by Salvador Allende, scrapes to victory, becoming Chile's first socialist government.

1971 Pablo Neruda wins the Nobel Prize.

1973 A military putsch led by General Augusto Pinochet (president from 1974 onwards) takes over, establishing a military dictatorship. Thousands of Allende's supporters are killed and thousands flee the country. Chile is faced with international isolation due to its human rights abuses.

1981 In a plebiscite two-thirds of the population vote in a constitution that limits Pinochet's term of office to 1989.

1987 Political parties are allowed again.

1988 A further period of office for Pinochet is blocked by a referendum vote.

1989 A center-left coalition (Concertación) wins a majority in a free nationwide vote.

1990–1994 Christian Democrat Patricio Aylwin heads the Chilean Government, marking the return to democracy.

1998 Pinochet retires as Army Commander in March and, in October, while visiting Britain, is arrested after Spain requests his extradition for human rights abuses against Spanish citizens.

2000 Released by the British Home Secretary, Jack Straw, on grounds of ill health, Pinochet returns to Chile. Socialist and Christian Democrat coalition leader, Ricardo Lagos, elected president.

2002 Charges against Pinochet are dropped on the grounds that he is mentally unfit to stand trial.

2004 Supreme Court ruling strips Pinochet of immunity from prosecution, with no right of appeal.

Cerro San Cristóbal

Route 1

Preceding pages:
Lake Llanquihue and Osorno

Santiago de Chile

The Cosmopolitan Capital *See map on page 24*

Plaza del Mulato Gil de Castro
and playing in Parque Forrestal

As you fly towards Santiago, to the east you'll see the endless pampas of Argentina, to the west the Pacific Ocean, and from north to south – as far as the eye can see – the majestic peaks of the Andes, dominated by the highest mountain on the continent, Aconcagua (6,959m/22,965ft).

The glass facades of this city of 5 million people flash in the sunshine as you approach. To the south and east you'll see the greener residential areas up on the slopes surrounding the center. Over one third of the country's population lives in Santiago, and almost 80 percent of its industrial production is located here, so the cityscape is often shrouded in smog, especially in winter. The symmetrical pattern of streets is interrupted by two hills, the Cerro San Cristóbal and Cerro Santa Lucía, with the Río Mapocho weaving its way between them to the coast. South of the riverside parks is the old part of the city with its old buildings, charmingly artistic corners and busy markets, packed with people and traffic. For evening entertainment there are all manner of music performances, discos, theaters and restaurants.

The area surrounding the city provides wine lovers with an opportunity to sample the fruits of vines that can be traced back to cuttings brought from France in the 19th century. To the southeast is the attractive Maipo Valley, the route for a drive into the Andes. There's also a day trip north to the ski region of Portillo, where a tunnel beneath the High Andes at 3,900m (12,870ft) emerges on the Argentine side, and provides a fine view of Aconcagua.

History

It was on the top of the 70m (230ft)-high Cerro Santa Lucía that Santiago was founded. In February 1541, the Spanish *conquistador* Pedro de Valdivia laid the foundation stone for a chapel, and the settlement that grew up on the western side of the hill was named Santiago del Nuevo Extremo, in honor of St James, patron saint of the Spanish Army. A few months later the town was destroyed by the Mapuches, but the Spanish rebuilt it undeterred. Many of the colonizers also moved into the uncharted south, where they founded eight settlements in swift succession. However, bitter resistance from the Indians forced them back north before the end of the 16th century.

Statue of Pedro de Valdivia in Plaza de Armas

It was only after this that Santiago gained significance as a capital, and within 50 years a total of 12 large churches had been built – their successors still stand on the same sites. But little else of this original cityscape survives. The entire city was destroyed by an earthquake in 1647, with the exception of the Iglesia de San Francisco; in 1730 the city was felled yet again, this time leaving just three buildings standing (all of which are museums today); and no fewer than 40 subsequent earthquakes mean that Chile's metropolis has almost completely lost its colonial face.

In the second half of the 19th century, however, after the War of the Pacific, when Chile gained the northern region with its mines and saltpeter reserves, the national economy prospered, and so did Santiago. French architects planned and built townhouses and public buildings. The result is that the skyline today is a mix of turn-of-the-20th-century pomp and extravagant skyscrapers. Santiago is the center of all important political, industrial, social and spiritual institutions in the country apart from the Congress, which convenes in Valparaíso *(see page 31)*.

City Tour 1 – The Center

Steps to Cerro Santa Lucía

The first tour of the city center comprises around 20 blocks and takes one day. Begin at the **Biblioteca Nacional ❶**, at Alameda 651. Built starting in 1913 in the French style, it is one of the oldest and largest libraries in South America.

If you walk via the monumental steps to the **Cerro Santa Lucía**, on a clear day you'll be rewarded with a magnificent view of the city, and if it's a summer evening there may even be a concert. At noon there's a thunderous cannon salute fired from the Terraza Caupolicán (which also features a statue of the Mapuche hero Lautaro, who led the Indian insurrection against the Spanish in the mid-1500s). The route continues up the hill past the Palacio Hidalgo, the remains of the fortress built by Pedro de Valdivia to protect the new settlement. From there you can take an elevator or walk back down. A word of warning: since thefts and muggings sometimes occur here, come only during the day.

The next stop on the tour is the neo-renaissance ★ **Basílica de la Merced ❷**, a church first built in 1549. The 18th-century baroque pulpit, built by German Jesuits near Santiago, has survived, as has the statue of the Virgen de la Merced which has been here ever since the basilica was built. The small **museum** (Tuesday to Friday 10am–1pm and 3–6pm, Saturday 10am–1pm) has some important items from Easter Island, including a rare *rongo rongo* inscription tablet (*see page 77*), the stone head of a fertility goddess and a choral book dating from 1680.

Teatro Municipal

In Calle Agustinas the elegant **Teatro Municipal ❸**, with its broad program of music and drama, is Santiago's most prestigious cultural venue and of architectural note too. The theater was built in 1857 to plans by Italian architect Joaquín Toesca; his other works include the cathedral, Basílica de la Merced and Palacio de la Moneda.

Walk northwards now along the extremely crowded Calle Estado to the ★ **Plaza de Armas**. On the right, at the beginning of the Calle Merced stands the ★ **Casa Colorada** (Tuesday to Friday 10am–6pm, Saturday 10am–5pm, Sunday and public holidays 11am–2pm). Built in the simple colonial style in 1769 for the Spanish governor, it became the residence of the country's first president in 1810. It has didactic models of the city, but few real exhibits. The ancient Plaza de Armas, or Weapons Square, is always a hive of activity: shoe-shiners, portrait painters,

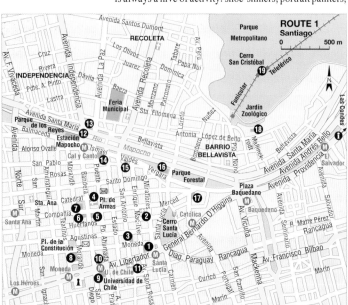

and Pentecostal preachers ply their trades, while candy and peanut vendors sell from their traditional *barquitos*, or little boats, and Pedro Valdivia looks down from his horse in the northeastern corner. On Friday and Sunday mornings and Thursday and Saturday afternoons, a very good police band plays on the bandstand on the eastern side of the plaza; the rest of the time, the bandstand is used for chess matches.

On the north side of the plaza is the municipalidad, or town hall, an elegant neoclassical building dating from 1790, built on the site of the former town hall and jail from colonial times. Adjoining it to the left is the ★ **Museo Histórico Nacional** (Tuesday to Sunday 10am–5.30pm) with a large range of exhibits documenting aspects of colonial life until the 20th century. The line of buildings is rounded off by the **main post office** (Monday to Friday 9am–5pm), a building that occupies the site of the old governor's palace.

The windows of the modern glass building on the corner reflect the ★ **cathedral ❹**, which makes the entire western end of the square very grand. This church was destroyed by earthquakes on three occasions, but always rebuilt in the original style conceived 200 years ago by Joaquín Toesca. The three-aisled interior contains a magnificent silver side-altar on the left. The **museum** (open Monday only 10.30am–1pm and 3–6pm) houses baroque artifacts from the burnt-down Jesuit church *(see below)* which were designed by monks in Bavaria.

The Cathedral

Go past a modern **sculpture** in honor of the aboriginal population to reach the Paseo Ahumada.

To the west of it, in Calle Bandera, the elegant walls of the former customs building, the ★ **Real Casa de la Aduana ❺**, house one of the best museums on the continent, the ★★ **Museo de Arte Precolombino** (Tuesday to Sunday 10am–6pm). This is the place to gain a memorable insight into the cultures of pre-Spanish America, from the continent's oldest ceramic collection (Ecuador, 3000–1500BC), through 3,000–4,000 year-old stone artifacts from Peru, to Peruvian Nazca textiles which are between 1,000 and 1,800 years old.

Indian monument

Real Casa de la Aduana

Immediately opposite, the interior courtyard of the **Tribunales de Justicia ❻** (Supreme Court) is illuminated by Art Nouveau domed windows. On the other side of Calle Compañía, the similarly styled former House of Congress is today occupied by the **Ministry of External Affairs ❼**, but was previously the site of the Jesuit headquarters, and later a church. The statue of the Virgin Mary in the grounds commemorates the 2,000 believers who were killed in 1863 when this church accidentally burned down, leading to the formation of the city's first fire brigade.

The Calle Morandé opens southwards into the broad **Plaza de la Constitución**. The largest building erected here during the 18th century by the Spanish crown was the **Palacio de la Moneda** , or Royal Mint, which served as the state president's residence from 1858 to 1958, and has since been the seat of the country's government. The south facade of this neoclassical building borders the large Avenida Libertador General Bernardo O'Higgins, the main street in the city center (familiarly known as the Alameda as it used to be an avenue of *álamo* or poplar trees).

Palacio de la Moneda

Two blocks farther east in the direction of the mountains, the central building of the **Universidad de Chile** ❾ contains not only numerous students but some fine neoclassical architecture as well.

On the other side of the street is the renowned and elegant **Club de la Unión** ❿, Latin America's oldest gentleman's club, whose lavishly decorated turn-of-the-20th-century rooms are decorated with numerous works of art by Chilean painters (sadly open to members only). At the rear, visitors can watch the noisy goings-on at the city's **Stock Exchange** (Monday to Friday 10.30–11.30am, 12.30–1.30pm and 4–4.30pm), founded in 1893.

The Alameda is rounded off by one of Santiago's best-known landmarks: the red-washed colonial ★★ **Iglesia de San Francisco** ⓫. Franciscan friars built the first church on this site in 1572, but the original adobe church was destroyed by an earthquake in 1883 and was replaced by a stone church (the nave of which survives) that was completed in 1612. The church's distinctive tower was added in 1860. One very special highlight here is the 450-year-old statue of the Virgen del Socorro, or Helping Maria, with its astonishingly moving and profound expression. Pedro de Valdivia placed this statue of Mary here after it had accompanied him on all his travels, firmly fixed to his saddle. The multicolored, gilt-coffered ceiling has several Arab elements. Next door to the church is an excellent ★★ **museum** (Monday to Saturday 10am–1pm and 3–6pm, Sunday and public holidays 10am–2pm) with paintings, statues and other artifacts dating from the colonial period, mainly of the Quito, Cusco and Potosí schools.

Iglesia de San Francisco and the Virgen del Socorro

City Tour 2 – Along the Río Mapocho

On the northern edge of the old town, alongside the former rail station, Estación Mapocho, the **Puente Cal y Canto** ⓬ spans the river. This fine bridge was originally built during colonial times, and has eight arches. Particularly eye-catching here are the imaginative funeral wreaths at the **Mercado de Flores** ⓭ flower market, and a few yards farther on the **fruit and vegetable market** contains the gamut of Chile's astonishingly diverse produce, from the warm subtropical areas to the colder northern regions. Always good-natured, the haggling here can get very lively.

The former **Estación Mapocho**, with its generously dimensioned iron structure that was designed by one of Chile's leading architects, Emile Jécquier, still has a rail station atmosphere, even though no trains have left here for the coast for years now. Today people come to attend exhibitions, concerts or theater performances. In 1872 a further steel and iron structure was built beside it: the magnificent, loftily domed English building that now contains the stalls of the ★★ **Mercado Central** ⓮, the city's central market. Its numerous delicacies can be tried out in the market's excellent restaurants.

In the Calle Esmeralda, farther to the east the adobe walls of the 18th-century **Posada del Corregidor** ⓯ (Monday to Friday 10am–7pm, Saturday 10am–2pm) have withstood earthquakes, and it now contains exhibitions.

In the shade of the old trees of the Parque Forestal is the ★ **Museo Nacional de Bellas Artes** ⓰, with the oldest art collection in South America comprising around 5,000 paintings and sculptures dating from the colonial period to the early 20th century. The neoclassical building also houses the **Museum of Contemporary Art** (closed in 2004 for restoration).

27

Museo Nacional de Bellas Artes

Go a short way along Cerro Santa Lucía and then turn left into Calle Merced. In Calle J Lastarria (on the right) is the easily missed entrance to the rewarding art center of ★ **Plaza del Mulato Gil de Castro** ⓱ with its artists', sculptors' and potters' workshops and studios, and also several good bookstores, theaters, galleries and the **Museo Arqueológico de Santiago** and the **Museo de Artes Visuales** with a small, but excellent collection of modern Chilean painting and sculpture (Tuesday to Sunday 10.30am–6.30pm). The small bohemian restaurants here are wonderfully peaceful.

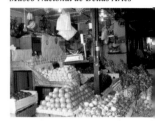

Mercado Central inside and out

City Tour 3 – Bellavista and Cerro San Cristóbal

The district of ★ **Bellavista** on the northern bank of the Río Mapocho has been an artists' quarter for years now, complete with narrow, tree-lined streets, small attractive squares, art galleries, excellent restaurants, workshops where you can see lapis lazuli being processed, and cafés serving delicious ice cream. This is a mixed residential and artistic neighborhood with considerable charm and interest.

Bellavista restaurant

A stroll through the streets of Mallinckrodt, Dardignac and A López de Bello should ideally end up at Calle Fernando Marqués de la Plata 0192: **La Chascona** ⑱ (built in 1955) was one of several unusual homes in Chile belonging to the poet Pablo Neruda *(see page 83)*, and is now a museum (Tuesday to Sunday 10am–5.45pm; guided tours). His library, with a vast collection of around 11,500 books including editions by Lord Byron and Edgar Allen Poe, can be seen here, together with several paintings by Chilean artists.

At Plaza Caupolicán you can take the rattling cableway (Monday to Friday 3–7pm, Saturday, Sunday and public holidays 10.30am–8pm) to the ★★ **Cerro San Cristóbal** (named after St Christopher by the Spanish because of the landmark it offered to travelers). There's a great view from up here across the High Andes and the entire city – particularly impressive at sunset. The 22.5m (74ft)-high, shiny white **Virgen de la Inmaculada Concepción** ⑲ extends her arms toward the city in a protective gesture.

There's a chair-lift *(teleferico,* Monday to Friday 10.30am–6.30pm, Saturday, Sunday and public holidays 10.30am–7pm, closed Monday mornings) above the hills to the east, where city dwellers flee to two swimming pools in the summer. There's also the **Enoteca** (daily 12.30pm–midnight), a good wine museum, with an excellent if rather expensive restaurant.

Elegant Shopping in the Suburbs

Parque Arauco shopping mall

At Plaza Baquedano, also known as the **Plaza Italia**, the city center comes to an end and Avenida B O'Higgins becomes Avenida Providencia. This leads on to the wealthy suburbs situated higher up the slope – the Barrio Alto. In these suburbs, along Avenida Kennedy, you will find two upmarket shopping centers with marble and brass malls: the **Alto Las Condes**, with its 240 elegant boutiques and the **Parque Arauco**, both of which can be reached by bus.

In the elegant suburb of Las Condes, at the end of Avenida Apoquindo (next to the church of Los Domínicos), is the craft village known as ★ **Los Graneros del Alba**. This is the best place to find local good-quality handicrafts. Here you can watch potters, painters, jewelry makers and sculptors at work.

Excursions from Santiago

The Maipo Valley

The picturesque Maipo Valley *See map on page 30*

A trip into the highly varied ★ **Cajón del Maipo** can be pleasantly rounded off with a visit to a vineyard. **San José de Maipo**, 50km (30 miles) southeast of Santiago, has a pretty colonial church, but the main reason people come here is the popular picnic sites. Also, anglers can catch trout or small *pejerreyes* (whitefish) in the streams of El Toyo and Coyanco here; and from September through April you can shoot the rapids on a raft.

The fascinating mountain world can best be explored from San Alfonso or San Gabriél. Between the simple thermal swimming baths of Baños Morales, 40km (24 miles) from San José de Maipo, and the more elegant Baños Colina (13km/8 miles away) stands 'Lo Valdés', the hotel of the German Andes Association, built in 1932 and the first-ever Andes mountain hut. It is open all year round, and a good starting point for hikes.

The church at San José

The orchards of the Aconcagua Valley (1–2 days)

Ruta 57 runs north of Santiago, parallel to the High Andes. After 52km (31 miles) you'll reach the monument commemorating the famous battle of Chacabuco, when the Chilean victory over the Spanish here on February 12 1817 marked the end of colonial rule.

On the other side of the Chacabuco tunnel, the barren landscape is transformed into numerous gentle, fertile orchards, and 15km (9 miles) farther on (toward San Felipe) you'll arrive at the **Santuario de Santa Teresa de los Andes**. This place of worship for the country's first saint is the center of a large Carmelite monastery complex.

The little town of San Felipe was a stopover on the old Inca route to the south. Around it the Río Aconcagua irrigates the land, making it ideal for growing all kinds

Aconcagua colors

of fruit (including kiwis, nectarines, peaches, plums and grapes) and vegetables.

Toward the east, the road heads for the mountains. The colorfully painted crockery and vases at the Cerámica Cala ceramic factory in **Los Andes** (Monday to Friday 9am–12.30pm, Saturday 10am–2.30pm) are popular throughout the country and available in all good stores.

Skiing at Portillo

The road now rises 1,000m (3,300ft) in a seemingly endless series of hairpin bends to reach the ski-lifts of **Portillo**, one of the most popular skiing centers in South America, located 50km (30 miles) outside Los Andes. At an altitude of 2,855m (9,420ft) there are pistes to suit every skier, plus the elegant Hotel Portillo *(see page 101)* which offers skiing packages (inclusive of lifts), plus every amenity for skiers, from crèches to massages. Snow cannons ensure the season lasts from June through September, and the region is also good for mountain hikes during summer.

Before and after the tunnel through the Andes massif – at an altitude of 3,900m (12,900ft) – are the Argentine border customs stations. On the Argentina side it's worth taking a small detour to the bronze statue of ★ **Cristo Redentor**, the symbol of peace between the two countries. The stunning view across the snow-capped peaks extends as far as Aconcagua, whose 4,000-m (13,000-ft) south face is a severe challenge for mountaineers.

The road runs another 200km (120 miles) down through the mountains in the valley of the **Río Mendoza**, and ends at the edge of the pampas in Mendoza.

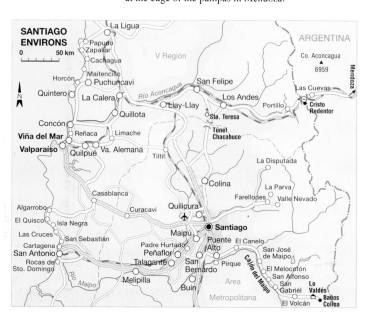

Viña del Mar and Valparaíso

Valparaíso and Viña del Mar, the largest harbor and the largest seaside resort in Chile respectively, have merged to form a twin city, which from a distance looks like an enormous amphitheater. The houses of Valparaíso lie high on the slopes of the north-facing, semicircular bay, where elevators have been rattling up and down for the past 100 years. Elegant Viña del Mar thrives all the year round with its long beach, casino, Palacio Vergara park and museum, many cafés, restaurants and shopping streets. The Sporting Club, which holds races every Wednesday, is popular with horse-racing fans. There are also around 20 more seaside resorts to the north and south of this twin city.

Valparaíso facades

It was in 1536 that the first Spaniards dropped anchor at Valparaíso, bringing food from Peru to support the campaign of conquest by Diego de Amagro. Slowly the town grew, but it was only after independence in the 19th century that Valparaíso developed into the most important center of trade and finance in Chile. The country's first banks, gas pipes and electric streetlights were installed here, together with the original stock exchange, tram system and telegraph and telephone network. Large trading firms made their headquarters in the town, and several of the mine-owners' magnificent residences are still partially open to the public as museums.

The harbor declined after the Panama Canal was built in 1914, but until then all the ships that rounded Cape Horn anchored in Valparaíso. In 1990, Congress was shifted here to give the city more significance and to decentralize government institutions from Santiago.

Plaza Sotomayor, Valparaíso

Valparaíso See map on page 33

It takes a day to see Valparaíso, on foot or by car. The trip over the hills parallel to the coast makes a delightful afternoon excursion, which will more than likely be rounded off by a stunning sunset over the ocean.

The lower part of the city, **El Plan**, starts by the harbor in the northwest. The piles of freight containers beside the massive ocean-going ships resemble building bricks, in stark contrast to the elegant passenger liners that drop anchor to the southeast, at Muelle Prat. Not far away, in Avenida Errázuriz which runs parallel to the bay, is Plaza Aduana with the Customs House, built 150 years ago and still in operation. Beyond it, an elevator climbs the steep slope as far as ★ **Cerro Artillería**. The rattling journey is definitely worth it for the fine view across the bay, and the former Naval Academy (Escuela Naval) is now the Museo Naval y Marítimo (Tuesday to Friday 9.30am–12.30pm and 2.30–6pm, Saturday, Sunday and public holidays, 10am–6pm), with its fascinating models of the fortifications of Valdivia, and of historic sailing ships.

Elevators connect the lower and upper cities

Tourist trap

Iglesia La Matriz

Leave Plaza Aduana and take Calle Bustamante to reach the main church of the city, **Iglesia La Matriz ❶**. It had to be rebuilt a fourth time in 1842 after destruction by fire and earth tremors, and until the beginning of the 19th century it was located directly next to the water. All ships were blessed here before leaving port until the land was reclaimed for El Plan, and the church lost its earlier significance. The highly revered 17th-century statue of Christ was a present from the Spanish Crown, and comes from Seville.

Plaza Echaurren, facing the sea, is surrounded by attractive buildings. It was the main square during colonial times, and several of the 100-year-old stores here still contain elegant wooden shelves covering entire walls. At the northwestern corner is the ★ **market hall ❷** with tiny restaurants where delicious specialties can be sampled. Go back now to the bottom of the hill and down Calle Serrano, as far as the Ascensor Cordillera, the oldest elevator in the city (1855). The first fort stood on the small rise here, but was destroyed during the 1822 earthquake. There are some interesting reconstructions of ships in the **Museo Cochrane ❸**, in a lovely colonial house named after a seafaring hero of the fight for independence.

The view from the top extends across the large ★★ **Plaza Sotomayor**, the heart of the city. At the foot of the hill, the present naval headquarters was built in 1910 as a summer residence for the state president (whose summer residence has been in Viña since 1930). In the middle of the square is the imposing memorial erected in honor of the heroic mariners at the sea battle of Iquique during the 1879–83 War of the Pacific *(see page 12)*, the most famous of whom – Arturo Prat, Ignacio Serrano and Carlos Condell – are buried in the mausoleum below it. Calle Prat leads eastwards from Plaza Sotomayor through the busy financial center with the stock exchange, banks and trading companies, then past the Edificio Turri with its stunning clock tower.

A walk around the ★ **upper town** with its *palacios* dating from the early days of lucrative saltpeter mining gets off to an atmospheric start with a trip in the Ascensor Peral (beside the law courts). The **Palacio Baburizza ❹** is an art museum, with a good selection of French, Spanish and Chilean paintings, but unfortunately it has been closed for renovation for several years and no date has yet been set for its re-opening. Walk eastwards up Pasaje Bavestrello to the Cerro Concepción, then follow Calle Urriola off to the right and continue a short way inside the old residential area as far as Calle Templeman. Here, in the direction of the sea, is the towerless Anglican church of **St Paul ❺**, built in neo-Gothic style in 1854. Farther east, toward the sea, is the high tower of the **Iglesia Luterana ❻** (late 19th-century), which has some attractive wooden arches and balconies.

The next stop on this walk is the Café Turri in the lower part of Calle Templeman, where you can enjoy excellent coffee and cake while appreciating the panoramic view. It is also a swanky restaurant. The Ascensor Concepción shortens the trip back down.

The route then goes via Avenida Esmeralda and on to Plaza Anibal Pinto with its old, established Café Riquet. Continue along Calle Condell, passing Plaza de la Victoria. The cathedral and one of the oldest libraries in the country, the **Biblioteca Severín ❼**, are side by side here.

The Ascensor Espíritu Santo will rattle you up the Cerro Bellavista, ending at the south side of the ★★ **Museo a Cielo Abierto**, a collection of murals painted on the sides of houses, some of them by leading Chilean artists *(see page 80)* such as Roberto Matta, Nemesio Antúnez, Mario Carreño and Mario Toral (whose work also adorns the Universidad de Chile subway station in Santiago) .

At the eastern end of Avenida Pedro Montt is the imposing **Congress Building**, opened in 1990 (Monday to Friday 9.30am–1pm and 3–5.30pm, guided tours tel. (329 505138), and opposite is the main bus station. Farther up the hill you'll reach Avenida Cintura, which winds its way westward, following every fold in the slopes. On Florida hill you can visit one of the houses that belonged to Pablo Neruda: **La Sebastiana**, at Calle Ferrari 692 (January and February Monday to Sunday 10.30am–6.50pm; March–December 10.10am–6pm, tel: 32-256606). Part of Neruda's eclectic collection of items acquired on his travels is housed here.

Edificio Turri

Viña waterfront

Palacio Presidencial

Casino Municipal

Viña del Mar

A casino, two pompous *palacios*, parks and a magnificent sandy beach are the main attractions of Valparaíso's young neighbor, the Garden City (Ciudad Jardín) and flourishing commercial center of Viña del Mar. Its important sights can be seen in a day, with the harbor area connected to the resort by 5.5km (3½ miles) of coastal highway.

Viña del Mar derives its name from a wine estate that was established in colonial times just north of the Estero Marga Marga, then a river flowing into the sea, now a dry estuary. During the mid-19th century, merchants from Valparaíso started to settle around the mouth of the river, and when the two towns were connected by railroad for the first time in 1855, Viña began to expand. After a catastrophic earthquake in 1906, many families moved to peaceful Viña del Mar from Valparaíso, and today 3.5km (2 miles) of sandy beach are the attraction for around a million visitors during peak vacation season.

The dry Marga Marga bed divides the city into two. The southern, older half has the railroad through it; the first *palacios* appeared here along Avenida Viana and Avenida Alvarez (north and south of the tracks respectively) in the second half of the 19th century, with their outbuildings and tradesmen's entrances facing on to Avenida Valparaíso. This boulevard was to develop into the most important and most elegant shopping street in Viña. It formed the old connecting route to the interior, intersecting the Panamericana and going on up the Aconcagua Valley via San Felipe and Los Andes, and separating Plaza José Francisco Vergara, with its stunning landscaped park *(see below)*, from the smaller Plaza Sucre.

From a rocky outcrop of the Cerro Castillo there is an excellent view across the sandy **Playa Caleta Abarca** to the sea. This beach can be reached from the center via Avenida Viana. Above the rock is the Tudor-style former *palacio* of the Ross family of merchants (now the Club Arabe), and farther uphill is the **Palacio Presidencial**, where Chile's presidents have spent their summers since 1930.

Sixty-year-old palm trees line the banks of the Estero Marga Marga. To the north of the Puente Casino you'll see the 1932 **Casino Municipal** (daily from 7pm), surrounded by shady green trees. Avenida Peru, formerly a stylish beach promenade with its *palacios*, known as *chalets* to the Chileans, is now a long line of skyscrapers. To the north it runs into Avenida San Martín, not far from the white sandy beaches of Acapulco and Mirasol, both uncomfortably crowded in January and February.

Farther inland along Avenida San Martín, the hotels and restaurants extend to the other side of Avenida Libertad. One block east of Libertad, on the corner of 4 Norte and 1 Oriente, is the ★ **Museo Arqueológico Fonck** (Tuesday to Friday 10am–6pm, Saturday, Sunday and public holidays 10am–2pm), housed inside the old *palacio* of the Délano family. The collections here range from fine silver Mapuche jewelry to valuable items from Easter Island, including an original *moai* (anthropomorphic statue forged from volcanic rock, *see page 76*).

In the same block, pay a brief visit to the **Palacio Carrasco**, entered via Avenida Libertad. This *palacio*, built in 1912, was used from 1930 to 1971 as a meeting place by the city fathers; today it's a cultural center.

Three blocks farther east is the **Palacio Rioja** (Quillota 214), with its attractive belle époque architecture, where important visitors to the city are often received. The *palacio* dates from the end of the 19th century, with the villa's original rooms preserved and on view (Tuesday to Sunday 10am–1.30pm and 3–5.30pm).

Inside Palacio Rioja

Across in the southern part of the city, two blocks south of Plaza José Francisco Vergara, is the most famous estate in Viña del Mar, the ★★ **Quinta Vergara**. Although the magnificent subtropical park here has been cultivated since 1843, the Venetian-style former home of the Vergara family house was only built after the earthquake of 1906. Today it houses the **Museo Municipal de Bellas Artes** (Tuesday to Sunday 10am–2pm and 3–6pm), containing numerous works by European and Chilean artists. A week-long song festival (*Festival de la Canción*) takes place in the park's *anfiteatro* every February. The rest of the year the park's grounds are open during daylight hours, and provide a peaceful sanctuary from Viña's hectic beach life.

Quinta Vergara grounds

Seaside resorts

Seaside resorts old and new line the bays of the Pacific like pearls along a chain. If you feel like taking a tour from

On the beach at Viña

Papudo

Santiago, drive along the Panamericana Norte as far as La Ligua and then via Papudo to the sea. The southern coastal resorts are reached from Santiago via Casablanca, an important wine-growing valley, or by the Autopista del Sol (Highway of the Sun). Both routes are day trips, ending in Viña-Valpo.

Viña northwards

Traveling northward from Viña del Mar, it's impossible to tell where the actual border is between Las Salinas (a popular beach) and the busy coastal resort of **Reñaca**. After a 12-km (7-mile) drive along the rocky coast, where numerous beach restaurants around the pretty Playa Cochoa are good places to stop, you'll reach the large bay of **Concón**. Before entering the town proper, why not do some sea-lion spotting at the Mirador de Lobos Marinos look-out point. In the part of town known as La Boca, where the Río Aconcagua reaches the Pacific, there are several excellent restaurants.

Quintero (pop. 19,000) is a well-sheltered resort on a peninsula and an important marina. The first ship anchored here in 1536, and its steersman, Alonso Quintero, gave the place its name. The next attractive resort is **Horcón**. Artists and craftsmen spend their vacations here, and can often be seen selling their work on the beach. Another 20km (12 miles) or so through the coastal ranges – above the old resort of Maitencillo – is the modern and elegant **Marbella Resort**. The hotel and restaurants here are good, and a wide range of sports activities is available.

The town along the coast is **Cachagua**, a small place with a long white beach and a family atmosphere. The elegant town of **Zapallar** grew up around the manor house belonging to the Ovalle family. The fine old villas

Humboldt penguins

and magnificent trees lend a particular charm to this place, with its semicircular bay, sandy beaches and modern facilities.

The northernmost seaside resort, ★ **Papudo**, is 10km (6 miles) away and 400 years old. As with the towns south of Valparaíso, earthquakes have not spared many old buildings here apart from the church and a few villas. The sheltered beach is ideal for all kinds of water sports.

Valparaíso southwards
On the way to the resorts south of Valparaíso you'll go inland first (along the highway as far as Casablanca), and then 30km (18 miles) through the coastal ranges as far as **Algarrobo**. The harbor and church were built in the middle of the 19th century, and the church contains a 17th-century black madonna that is considered very valuable. Swimming, windsurfing and sailing are popular here, even though the water temperature in summer hardly ever exceeds 15°C (60°F). The slopes are covered with attractive villas, and the marina is a favorite venue for regattas.

High summer in Algarrobo

After 4km (2½ miles) of romantic, rocky coast you'll reach **El Quisco**, which livens up at night with its many popular nightclubs. The next attraction is ★ **Isla Negra**, which despite the name is not an island but a beach resort. The biggest attraction for visitors is Pablo Neruda's house, built in 1960 (Tuesday to Sunday 10am–2pm and 3-6pm; in summer, 10am–8pm; guided tours only lasting around an hour tel: 35-461284); it was the great poet's favorite place, and he is buried in the grounds. The house itself is unremarkable, but contains examples of Neruda's literary work and a fine range of ships' figureheads and numerous other memorabilia.

After several smaller towns such as Las Cruces and San Sebastián, the bay of ★ **Cartagena** (pop. 15,000) is a good place for a swim. In the early 20th century it was an exclusive resort with luxurious villas. It was here that the poet Vicente Huidobro *(see page 82)* lived and died, and the railroad line to Santiago was opened in 1919. Since then Cartagena has been the most popular seaside resort for Chile's middle and working classes.

The second-largest harbor town of the coastal region and the country's busiest port is **San Antonio** (pop. 126,000). At the fish market here you can buy everything from soft and delicious *congrio* (kingklip) to sea urchins.

Our trip along the southern resorts ends at **Rocas de Santo Domingo** on the southern side of the Río Maipo estuary. The highlights here include an old golf club and some magnificent holiday homes perched high on the rocks amid beautiful parks, or along the long beach where the west wind whips up the surf 360 days a year.

The coast at Rocas de Santo Domingo

Oficina Humberstone

Route 2

The Great North

Arica – Putre – Lauca National Park – Salar Surire – Iquique – Antofagasta – Calama – San Pedro de Atacama *See map opposite*

In the infinite north of Chile, brilliant blue sky lies above bare, shimmering brownish-red mountains, snow-clad volcanoes and white lakes of salt. The landscape is alien to human life, but man has been attracted here all the same by the wealth of mineral resources. The best starting-point for an exploratory trip through the region is Arica, a harbor town and also a good place to get gasoline before driving to the dizzying heights above.

Atacama salt desert

In the middle of The Great North, El Norte Grande, deserted and ghostly estates stand as reminders of past wealth. It was here that saltpeter was discovered, processed and sold on the world market. The regional capital of Iquique is full of magnificent buildings testifying to the area's former wealth. The southernmost stop on the route is Antofagasta, a starting-point for tours to Chuquicamata, the Atacama salt desert, and the Valley of Geysers 4,300m (14,107ft) above sea level – the driest region on earth.

Planning and organizing trips along 'Chile's bootlace' is difficult. The Arica–Putre–Lago Chungará route can be done as a day trip returning to Arica (400km/240 miles). Those feeling fit for an altitude of 4,300m (14,100ft), and in possession of four-wheel-drive vehicles (in case of breakdown in this remote area, you should always travel with another vehicle in convoy), have two possibilities: either a trip from Putre via Guallatiri to Salar Surire with an overnight stay in Putre, or from Surire past the

monumental mountain scenery through the Isluga National Park via Enquelga to Iquique and then to the coast.

As far as travel times are concerned, Arica–Putra–Lago Chungará–Salar Surire–Arica takes two to three days and is around 500km (300 miles); Arica–Putre–Salar Surire–Isluga–Iquique takes three to four days and is around 640km (384 miles). The following are essentials for tours at high altitude: get your car ignition adapted before you leave, take along enough gasoline for the whole trip (there are no gas stations after Arica), and enough food and oxygen along with sleeping bags so that you can overnight in the car, in temperatures as low as -10°C (14°F).

★ **Arica**, the northernmost town in Chile, is protected to the south by the Morro, a steep wall of rock above the Pacific and the symbol of the town. Arica lies in a bay which turns into Peruvian desert farther north and extends eastwards through the barren mountains to the fertile Azapa valley. South of the Morro there are several large and inviting sandy beaches for swimming such as El Laucho and La Lisera.

Until 1880 Arica belonged to Peru, which was forced to cede it in the War of the Pacific in the 1880s. That was when Bolivia lost Antofagasta, its only access to the sea. To make up for this, Chile built the Arica–La Paz and Antofagasta–La Paz railroad lines, and Peru and Bolivia were accorded special rights in both harbors. Arica gained its prominence, after the viceroy was installed in Peru (1569–1824), for shipping silver from Potosí in Bolivia; this was the largest town in the Western world at that time with 160,000 inhabitants – only slightly less than Arica has today. At first the silver was transported over long distances by mule to the ships; from 1913 a railroad has covered the 416km (250 miles) from Arica to La Paz (a 'fast' journey is an 11-hour slog, while the slow train takes a lumbering 20 hours). If you have a 'heart for heights', don't miss the magnificent trip through the mountain landscape, which culminates at a high pass 4,257m (14,000ft) above sea level.

In Arica it's worth taking a quick taxi ride to the ★ **Morro** for the fantastic view it provides of the harbor, the many fishing boats, the town and far into the green Azapa valley. In 1879 the decisive battle in the War of the Pacific against Peru was fought on the rise here.

At the foot of the Morro, a palm-lined avenue leads to the invitingly restful Parque Baquedano. The rail station was built in 1913, and outside it

Cathedral of San Marco

Cemetery at Putre and Aimará woman

is a disused German locomotive with the inscription '1924, Maschinenfabrik Esslingen'. The former customs house beside it is now a cultural center. A few steps farther on is the striking neo-Gothic cathedral of ★ **San Marco,** whose iron construction was designed by Gustav Eiffel in Paris in 1868, then assembled in Arica.

In the **Pueblo Artesanal** in the Plaza las Gredas you can not only buy musical instruments but also hear folk music performances (Friday and Saturday 9.30pm).

There's a good detour at this point to the very interesting ★★ **Museo Arqueológico de Arica** (daily 10am–6pm; January and February 9am–8pm, tel: 58-205551) in **San Miguel de Azapa**. The town is 13km (8 miles) from the coast in the fertile Azapa Valley, where the best olives in Chile are grown. This museum provides a fascinating cross-section of the various tribes who inhabited this region during pre-Spanish times.

For an excursion into the mountains, start on the surfaced road that runs northward from the town. Turn east off it along Ruta 11 into the ★ **Valle Lluta**, which with its irrigated fertile landscape is quite a contrast to the stony, rocky desert. At kilometer marks 13 and 15 there are some striking ★ earth 'paintings' of llamas and people. These strange dark shapes etched out of the pale ground are an enigma to archeologists *(see page 44* for the best-preserved example, Geoglifos de Pintados).

The road goes through **Poconchile** 35km (21 miles) from Arica. Take a look at the walled cemetery here: its stone crosses stand behind an old adobe church, right in the middle of the desert sand. At kilometer 75 there's a vast field of impressive candelabra cacti; their thick stems can grow as high as 5m (17ft).

At kilometer 140 you'll reach the town of ★ **Putre**, located 3,500m (11,550ft) above sea level. The Hotel Las Vicuñas is a good place to take a break, and enjoy a cup of coca-leaf tea to combat potential altitude problems. After that you can take a brief stroll through this 400-year-old town whose name translates as 'sadness'. With spindles in their hands, Indian women can be seen driving their llamas and alpacas to the large compound near the hotel, from where the animals are exported all over the world. They belong to the Aimará tribe and still speak the ancient language of their forefathers who thousands of years ago made the trek from Lake Titicaca to northern Chile.

The excursion to ★ **Lago Chungará** in the **Parque Nacional Lauca** is best started in the early morning. That's when the animals near the trails and the lakes are at their most active, including the vicuña (cud-chewing mammals similar to the llama), which is thriving now that it is a protected species. Between the rocky outcrops you'll see

clumps of light-green yareta *(Azorella compacta)*, a protected plant with a diameter of up to 1m (3ft). It takes centuries to grow, and hardens with age – which is why so much of it was used as firewood until it became protected. Emerald-green Lago Chungará lies at an altitude of 4,500m (14,850ft), and wildlife here includes flamingos, herons, large coot, geese, and ducks. The viscacha *(Lagostomus maximus)*, a relative of the chinchilla, also lives in this region.

Las Payachatas (above) and yareta specimen

Snow-capped volcanoes provide the majestic backdrop to the east: the 'twins' *(Las Payachatas)* Pomarape (6,240m/20,590ft) and Parinacota (6,330m/1,320ft), the Quisiquisini (5,480m/18,080ft) and the highest, Nevado de Sajama (6,520m/21,500ft). The route now leads to the picturesque pre-Spanish village of ★ **Parinacota**. Small houses are grouped around the 200-year-old adobe church, with its frescoed interior. Surrounded by a low clay wall, with its two-story bell-tower at one corner and a cross beneath a stone baldachin (canopy), the church is actually built on sand. Two small crosses on its reed-thatched roof brave the wind and rain. The blue portal, not even the height of a man today, is surrounded by ornamented red stone. The whole village seems deserted, and thick padlocks can be seen on many of the doors. Young people have left for the cities, and the old come back only for religious festivals and the carnival, spending the rest of the year with their llama and alpaca herds up in the pastures. They mark their animals' ears with colored strands of wool, and control them with short sharp whistling sounds. Strangers are eyed very cautiously; if you're relaxed and friendly, people soon lose their shyness, but don't forget they believe you're taking away part of their soul – and their animals' souls too – if you photograph them.

With a sturdy automobile and good equipment you can continue this journey of discovery southwards now. Cross

A vicuña looks on

The Salar Surire

the asphalt highway and stay on the rough track, on which, a few kilometers later, there's a turn-off to the village of **Choquelimpie** with its gold and silver mine (now closed to the public).

In the **Reserva Nacional Las Vicuñas** cars have to do quite a bit of alpaca, llama and vicuña dodging on their way south. The track crosses the Río Lauca (make sure you test the depth of the water before proceeding), and after another 30km (18 miles) you'll reach the 50 houses that make up **Guallatiri**, not far from the smoking volcano of the same name. This pre-Spanish village also has a 17th-century adobe church, whitewashed this time, plus bell-tower, surrounded by a wall.

The landscape now becomes infinitely vast and lonely, and the route crosses the Río Lauca yet again before branching east 30km (18 miles) farther on at the ★ **Salar Surire** (124km/74 miles from Putre). This salt lake is teeming with flamingos and wild geese, and on the barren banks you'll see groups of vicuñas grazing – and maybe even that small South American version of the ostrich known as the ñandu, a shy beast that runs away at the slightest unfamiliar thing.

Borax, used primarily in medicine, is mined on the southern bank of the Salar. If the route southward is passable (the police station on the north bank of the lake can provide information on road conditions), leave early in the morning in the shadow of the high mountains, passing the Volcán Isluga, as far as Enquelga (96km/57 miles), an Aimará Indian village. Isluga, 6km (3½ miles) to the south, is a *pueblo ritual* like Parinacota, where the inhabitants are primarily herders, assembling only for religious festivals. **Colchane** has food stores and also a police station for information; this border station with Bolivia is a mere 3,730m (12,240ft) above sea level.

To travel through the valley that many Chileans consider the finest in the Andes, you have to go back to Enquelga and then head west (24km/14 miles) to **Mauque**. Lakes, pastureland and mountains combine to form utterly breathtaking scenery. A few kilometers beyond Mauque, the route branches off to the southeast (left) and leads to the international highway 12km (7 miles) later.

At this point you are 180km (108 miles) from Iquique. If you go from Arica direct, the 316km (190 miles) to Iquique can be covered by car or bus (four to five hours) on the Panamerican Highway (Ruta 5), or in less than an hour by plane.

★ **Iquique** (pop. 215,000) is a happy, busy and noisy place these days – ironically, since its name means 'silence'. When Iquique was founded in 1730 it was Bolivian, and a trading center for silver from the mine in

Huantaja; 100 years later it became important for the first saltpeter exports. Buildings dating from the city's heyday in the late19th century include the fine neoclassical ★ **Teatro Municipal** on leafy Plaza Arturo Prat, the three-story clock tower, and the Moorish-looking ★ **Centro Español**. A few blocks to the south of the latter is the ★ **Palacio Astoreca**, on the corner of Baquedano and O'Higgins (Tuesday to Friday 10am–1pm and 4–7pm, weekends 11am–2pm), a mansion with opulent Georgian-style rooms, works by local artists and a large shell collection. The palm-lined Avenida Baquedano is bordered by fine wooden *palacios*, with pillared arcades, balconies and small look-out towers called *miradores*.

Downtown Iquique

The export of fishmeal, of which Chile is an important producer, brought prosperity to Iquique in the 1970s. In 1985 a massive duty-free shopping center opened in the north of the city, and has also been an important source of revenue. Just 1km (⅔ mile) north of the city limits, on a rocky outcrop by the sea, you can see a bronze statue of a mariner built in honor of those who died in the sea battle of May 21 1879. There's an excellent panoramic view from here, and out in the waves you'll see the buoy marking the location where the Chilean ship *Esmeralda* sank during the War of the Pacific. The Cavancha peninsula in the south of the city has all the most popular sandy beaches, the best hotels and modern villas.

43

Day trips from Iquique

A trip into the desert from Iquique reveals an amazing mixture of weird emptiness and bustling oases: beyond old saltpeter mining centers there are refreshing springs in the oasis towns of the Andes foothills; and in between is the **Pampa del Tamarugal**, a vast forest of Tamarugo trees that can grow up to 20m (66ft) tall.

Tamarugo trees and the interior of Iquique's Palacio Astoreca

Santa Laura saltpeter mine

From the sea there's a well-surfaced road that winds its way inland to around 600m (1,980ft), where an observation point will give you a breathtaking view across Iquique and the gigantic sand dune known as El Dragón (The Dragon). Another 30km (18 miles) farther on, on the right, is the oldest saltpeter mine, **Santa Laura**, which was in operation from 1890 to 1910, but today lies deserted, the wind blowing eerily through dilapidated wooden planks.

Until around 1920 saltpeter (potassium nitrate) was used as a fertilizer and raw material for explosives, and at one point Chile was exporting three million tons of it a year. But in 1918 the Germans began manufacturing calcium nitrate from atmospheric nitrogen, and this was soon in great demand. At the moment only two of the old mines are still in operation, María Elena and Pedro de Valdivia, but since world demand for saltpeter is increasing again, new mines have been opened. A few kilometers north of Santa Laura, at the intersection with the Panamericana, is **Oficina Humberstone**, where saltpeter was mined for almost 100 years. Now a ghost town, it is the easiest of the former saltpeter centers to explore, and its theater, church and market have been restored.

Before turning off eastwards from the Ruta 5 to the oases of Matilla and Pica, travel 2km (1½ miles) west from the main highway to the ★ **Geoglifos de Pintados**. These pre-Columbian earth drawings were produced either by scratching away the layer of light stone above a darker lower one, or by placing dark patterns on top of a large, light-colored base. The *geoglifos* depict men, animals and various symbols, and were probably created for a religious purpose, though they may also have functioned as signposts. Their date of origin has been fixed at anywhere between 1000 and 1400. Drawings like these can be found

Oficina Humberstone: church interior

Geoglifos de Pintados

at several places on the eastern slopes of the coastal ranges, as well as in the Lluta and Azapa valleys *(see page 40)*.

The Matilla and Pica oases (36km/21 miles from Ruta 5) are closely linked historically. The springs at Pica made it a paradise in the desert, and the Inca route southwards also passed via here. The *conquistadores* Diego de Almagro and Pedro de Valdivia stopped over in Pica.

After Iquique was established, many Spanish families moved to the small town of Pica because of its mild weather, and started a wine industry. The tools they used for wine-making can be seen in **Matilla** beside the church. Sand storms prevented further wine production at the beginning of the 20th century, and then the water was diverted to Iquique, depriving this place of its life support. The parish church, rebuilt after an earthquake in 1887, and later lovingly restored, was sadly again extensively damaged, like much of the area, by a severe earthquake in June 2005. The altar, which has survived, dates from the original colonial building: note the striking *Last Supper* with its life-sized figures.

La Tirana comes alive

Although **Pica** (pop. 4,500) no longer survives from winemaking alone, it once exported wine to Peru and Bolivia and today it uses the large area of irrigated land to grow mangos, guavas and citrus fruit, especially the small *limones de Pica*, considered the best for making Chile's national cocktail, *pisco sour*. On the edge of the town, wonderfully clear springs fill small bathing pools with water, one of the most popular of which is the Cocha Resbaladero (daily 8am–9pm). As in Matilla, the main square has a church dating from the end of the 19th century, which also contains a *Last Supper*.

On the way back to Iquique you'll pass **La Tirana**, 10km (6 miles) and the last stop before Ruta 5. This tiny village comes alive between July 12 and 18 every year. From the entire Great North people converge wearing magnificent costumes and carved devil-masks, whereupon much dancing in honor of Chile's patron saint, La Virgen del Carmen, takes place. Iquique is another 70km (42 miles) from here.

To cover the 490km (300 miles) between Iquique and Antofagasta you have a choice of routes: along Ruta 5 across the plateau between the coastal ranges and the Andes, past the saltpeter centers of Pedro de Valdivia and María Elena, or along the picturesque Ruta 1, which has good places for swimming and is 80km (48 miles) shorter.

After 188km (112 miles) you'll reach the provincial capital, **Tocopilla** (pop. 31,000), which was founded as a harbor for saltpeter export 150 years ago and has now become the site of an electricity works that provides the Chuquicamata mine *(see page 47)* and the local saltpeter and fishmeal factories with power.

Antofagasta – Center of Mineral Wealth

One of the most varied of our suggested tours in Chile lasts five days. The sights in the harbor city of Antofagasta, the magnificent Portada rock included, take half a day to cover. Calama, 200km (120 miles) away, is a good starting-point from which to visit one of the world's largest open-cast copper mines, Indian villages, the oasis village of San Pedro de Atacama with its ancient past, the mysterious and ghostly salt mountains, the salt desert – where even the tiniest drop of perspiration dries instantly in temperatures of around 40°C (105°F) – and the highest geysers in the world at El Tatio. The route is around 1,000km (600 miles) long, but all these attractions lie along it.

The Portada rock

Antofagasta (pop. 313,000) is the fourth-largest city in Chile. The local economy is based on the shipping of copper and saltpeter and the services the city provides to the mining industry. The streets run chessboard-like from the sea eastwards to the dry mountain slopes, where most of the population lives. Everyone remembers the awful rainstorm of 1991 with a shudder: it caused a horrific mudslide, killing over 100 people and burying an entire suburb.

The neo-classical houses dating from the heyday of saltpeter production – many of them in dire need of renovation – are a typical feature of the city center. The **Plaza Colón** has an attractive clock tower, and its resemblance to Big Ben in London is no coincidence – it was a present to the city from the British colony here. Buildings dating from the early 20th century can be seen in Calle Baquedano near the harbor: the historic railroad station *(estación de ferrocarriles)*, where the goods trains laden with copper from Chuquicamata mine rumble by regularly; and the pretty ★ **Museo Regional** (Monday to Friday 9am–5pm, weekends 11am–2pm), housed inside the former customs office (1866, the oldest building in town), with exhibitions about the area's natural and political history. On the opposite side of the street are the harbor authority and coastguard buildings, both dating from around 1900.

The disused 1872 quay can still be seen at the harbor, a reminder of the time when saltpeter was sent all over the world from here. On the northern edge of the bay is the fish market, which has a large selection and is definitely worth a visit. Hungry pelicans enjoy the catch too.

On the southern edge of the town are the remains of the fortress-like silver foundry **Huanchacha**, which was in operation from 1888 to 1898. To avoid any silver being lost through theft, the ore from the mountain was carried to the coast on mules before being smelted and purified there. The symbol of the town rises up from the water 16km (10 miles) to the north of it: La Portada, a picturesque natural rock portal.

46

Downtown Antofagasta

Huanchacha remains

Old cultures and bizarre landscapes

High noon near San Pedro

Out in the desert, three hours by bus or half an hour by plane from Antofagasta, and at 2,250m (7,400ft) above sea level lies the dormitory town of **Calama** (pop. 137,000), where two-thirds of the workforce at the Chuquicamata copper mine are housed. The town itself is unattractive, but a useful base for trips through the surrounding region. From the main square in Calama shared taxis travel every 20 minutes to ★★ **Chuquicamata**, one of the world's largest copper mines, operated by the state-owned Codelco. The first bars of copper left here in May 1915, and today, it still produces around 600,000 tons of 99.9-percent pure copper each year. Chile as a whole provides 35 percent of the world's copper, 5 percent of which is produced by Chuquicamata alone. Half-day tours of the mine are available.

47

The first excursion destination in the Antofagasta region is ★ **Chiu Chiu**. Hunters and gatherers settled here in 1000BC on the Loa, Chile's longest river. The Loa is also the only river in the north to reach the sea (some 1,000km/600 miles farther on); all the others drain away into the desert or take an underground route to the Pacific. The Incas and later the Spanish valued the pastureland here, and Chiu Chiu has always been located on an important trading route. Today it is surrounded by alfalfa and vegetable fields, and the inhabitants go to the river each December – before and after they've shorn their llamas and alpacas – to wash their valuable animals.

Chiu Chiu church

The ★ **church**, with its 1.2-m (4-ft) thick adobe walls, was built in 1675. The wood in the clay-and-straw roof comes from a local tree called the *chañar*. The beams are held together with alpaca sinew, and paneled with cactus-wood strips. Statues of saints and small altars decorate the attractive interior.

Atmospheric Ayquina and Caspana cemetery

A few kilometers east of the village, on the right, there's a round, blue water-hole 600m (1,980ft) deep and 100m (330ft) across. This is an artesian well, where water from the High Andes comes up from far below ground. Another 35km (21 miles) farther on is **Ayquina**, another *pueblo ritual*. Very few people actually live in the stone houses, since most are out herding their llamas and alpacas; they come back here only now and then for festivals.

It's another 16km (10 miles) from here to ★ **Caspana**, where the desert forms a plateau, into which a life-giving river has cut its way. The Aimará Indian settlement lies on its banks, with an older upper part and more modern lower section and flower and vegetable terraces in between. A museum in the lower village documents local history, and local craft products can be bought in a store: spinning, weaving and knitting are all a source of income for the inhabitants. The two streets in the upper section are lined by stone houses, all huddled together with clay roofs and crosses (to ward off evil spirits). The simple adobe church (1641) has a pleasant interior with fine altarpieces.

On the way back to Calama, just before Chiu Chiu, you can travel 8km (5 miles) northward into the Loa Valley. The **Pukará de Lasana** fortress nestles between steep rocky walls, and has guarded the valley since the 12th century.

A very attractive destination in the Calama region is the village of San Pedro de Atacama, easily reached along 100km (60 miles) of good road. After around 35km (21 miles) you'll see a bright-green pimiento tree *(Schinus molle)* at the side of the road with a sign beside it saying *Dáme Agua* – 'Give me water!' People driving by greet it and make the sign of the cross in blessing, and anyone who has any water gives some to the tree.

Pimientos are native to Peru, and quite a few can be found in the desert. They provide plenty of shade, reach a maximum height of 10–15m (35–50ft) after 20 years, and many are centuries old.

The last barrier on the desert road from Calama to the southeast is the **Cordillera de la Sal**, or Salt Mountain. From the top of the pass (2,500m/8,250ft) there's a great view into the green valley with San Pedro and its river. To the east you can see the chain of majestic volcanoes, with Licancabur (5,916m/19,520ft) in the foreground, the holy mountain of the Atacameños and later of the Incas, whose slopes drop 3,600m (11,880ft) from a flat top.

The two thousand or so inhabitants of the peaceful oasis village of ★★ **San Pedro de Atacama** (2,438m/8,045ft) live in low clay houses on sandy streets. Hunter-gatherers settled in this region around 12,000 years ago, and this is also where the Atacama culture of the Andean desert oases originated. When the Spanish passed by here on their way from Cusco southwards, they found 15 family communities *(ayllos)* who shared the oasis land and the water – some of these still exist today.

At the small market in the main square, the locals sell their products made from wool and wood. The church, over 400 years old, is also in this square, its thick adobe walls, a straw and clay thatched roof and a stepped bell-tower all shining brilliant white behind a wall. The ceiling inside is carved from cactus wood, and the statues of the saints are charmingly naive.

San Pedro church and interior

49

The ★★ **Museo Arqueológico Padre Le Paige** (Monday to Friday 9am–noon and 2–6pm; weekends 10am–noon and 2–6pm) is of particular importance. From 1955 till his death in 1980, the Belgian Jesuit priest who gives the museum its name was one of the first people to research the Atacama Indian culture. The museum had its humble beginnings in 1963, but now contains around 380,000 exhibits which include mummies, pots, materials, small wooden trays and gold. It provides a comprehensive insight into the 11,000-year-old pre-Spanish culture of northern Chile.

Padre Le Paige

North of San Pedro is the large, 800-year-old fortress *(pukará)* of **Quitor**, high above the river. A semicircular tower lies at the center of this bastion, which was built during the time of the Incas. The stones used are of different sizes – an unusual feature.

Back to the west of San Pedro, the Cordillera de la Sal is also worth closer inspection. Here, the shadows in late-afternoon in the ★★ **Valle de la Luna** (south of the Calama–San Pedro road) or the **Valle de la Muerte** (north of the road) – both 10km (6 miles) from San Pedro – are fascinating. The reddish-gray mountains, valleys and peaks of solidified salt and clay turn the landscape into

Salar de Atacama

Toconao local

El Tatio geyser

something out of a movie, especially if there happens to be a full moon. The whole region once used to be a huge lake, the bottom of which rose and dried.

An excursion to the ★★ **Salar de Atacama** salt lake south of San Pedro is also highly recommended. After 36km (21 miles) you'll reach the oasis of **Toconao**. Here the church tower is separate from the church itself, and stands in the middle of the pleasantly shady main square. Over time, the wind has blown several miniature sand dunes over the graves in the small cemetery at the edge of the village.

A few kilometers farther on the road turns off into the salt lake and becomes a track. All around you'll see about 3,000 sq km (1,160 sq miles) of encrusted salt where the water has evaporated to leave sharp-edged points and peaks. The wind has covered the salt with sand, but here and there it still shines a brilliant white. There is actually a lake beneath this nasty-looking carpet, and part of it forms the Laguna Chaxa – a nature reserve and popular haunt of three species of flamingo. The Laguna is also preserved by artesian pressure and a subterranean connection with the High Andes. Zero humidity and 40°C (105°F) of heat keep the salt crust tense and brittle, and you'll hear it cracking incessantly.

Not far away, the **Volcán Lascar** (5,154m/17,008ft) is an active volcano and has a plume of smoke above it. In 1993 its lava was thrown up to heights of 15km (10 miles) during a fierce eruption. At the southern end of the salt lake a new industry has sprung up: lithium mining. Forty percent of the world's lithium reserves are here; the alkaline metal is used in medication and also in mineral water production.

From San Pedro several pass roads lead through the magnificent mountain scenery to Argentina and Bolivia. The **Jama Pass** is the best for driving, but visitors should also enquire locally about a possible excursion to the **Laguna Verde**, over the border in Bolivia. Dominated by the cone of Licancabur, this turqoise lake is home to a rich variety of birdlife and is a wonderful place from which to savor the drama and isolation of the Andes.

Anyone who would like to experience the ★ **geysers** at **El Tatio** in their full glory will have to get up early in the morning. Four-wheel-drive vehicles set off while it's still dark up the Cuesta del Diablo, or Devil's Slope, through riverbeds and past several volcanoes (some of which are active and some extinct) until they reach an altitude of 4,321m (14,260ft), where you'll see an open valley with steaming waterholes. The steam rises high into the air in the gray light of dawn. Once the sun is up, however, its warm rays tend to make the spectacle rather less impressive.

Route 3

La Silla observatory

The 'Small North' – Where Nature is Friendlier

Copiapó – Vallenar – La Serena – Andacollo – Valle del Elqui – Coquimbo – Parque Nacional Fray Jorge – Ovalle

Between Copiapó and La Serena, the landscape changes its appearance. In the north, the barren desert is lent a dash of color by the light green of the vineyards – but it's only via drip irrigation that the grapes can ripen here around Christmas time. If it rains – and it only rains, if ever, in the winter – the brown of the desert is suddenly transformed, and a beautiful carpet of flowers covers the whole land, even after a decade of drought. The sky is almost always completely clear, day and night, which is why the three most important observatories in the southern hemisphere are all located here: Las Campanas, La Silla and El Tololo.

The 8km (5 miles) of beach in La Serena and a lively, colorful city center with a vast variety of pottery, fruit and textiles make the town a great place to stay. The fertile Valle del Elqui in the east has magnificent landscape, and was the homeland of the only Latin American woman to have won the Nobel Prize in Literature (1945), Gabriela Mistral *(see page 82)*. As you continue south, natural and cultural experiences await in the shape of the rainforest of Fray Jorge, and the mysterious ancient petroglyphs in the Valle del Encanto.

The 566km (340 miles) from Antofagasta to Copiapó can be covered only along Ruta 5, either in a car or a luxury bus (and taking seven to eight hours). The stretch from Copiapó via Vallenar to

Copiapó: green land

La Serena (340km/204 miles), with a half-day detour (132km/79 miles) to one of the two observatories of La Silla or Las Campanas, requires two days to complete if you want to experience all the attractions along the route through the desert. La Serena and the Valle del Elqui (210km/126 miles), with an excursion to the observatory at El Tololo (76km/45 miles), can be covered in two days, while it takes just one day to explore La Serena, the coastal resorts and the Valle del Encanto (400km/240 miles).

The capital of this administrative region, ★ **Copiapó** (pop. 126,000), means 'green land' and is the name given to the area by the Indians. Since several rivers meet up to the east of the city, the valley is especially fertile. Not only did the Incas stop here on their way southward but also the Spanish explorers Diego de Almagro and Pedro de Valdivia on their campaigns of conquest. Copiapó reached its peak of prosperity when the silver deposits were discovered in its hinterland. The British and Americans built the first railroad line in South America here in 1855, connecting Copiapó with the Pacific harbor at Caldera.

52

Not far from the Palacio Viña de Cristo, the most elegant building in the city, built in 1860 to European designs (Monday to Friday 8am–7pm), you can see the first-ever locomotive on display in the university campus on the Avenida Copayapu Norte.

The main square, the **Plaza Prat**, was planted with 84 pimiento trees 120 years ago. These gnarled giants now surround a fountain, providing shade for graceful marble figures representing the seasons. The **cathedral** (after Mass Monday to Saturday 7pm; Sunday 8.30am, noon and 7.30pm) has several neoclassical stylistic elements, and its wooden construction, which dates from the middle of the 19th century, is typical of this region. The double walls, however, are unique in Chile, and you can walk along the 1.3-m (4-ft) gap between them.

Museo Mineralógico

If you cross Plaza Prat diagonally from the cathedral you reach the ★ **Museo Mineralógico** (Monday to Friday 10am–1pm and 3.30–7pm, Saturday 10am–1pm) on the corner of Rodriguez and Colipi. With over 13,000 exhibits, it's the most comprehensive museum of this kind in Chile, providing an excellent overview of minerals including meteorites from the Atacama Desert and yellow arsenic blends from the silver mines.

The region around Copiapó is known today for its delicious grapes. Every plant in this vast area is watered by computer control, and in September piece workers come from all over Chile to prune and tie back the plants. The harvest then reaches international markets for Christmas.

Vallenar, 150km (90 miles) from Copiapó, becomes an important starting-point for tours whenever the desert is in bloom. Otherwise, apart from some fine old trees, the town has no attractions. On the journey south, 96km (59 miles) from Vallenar, a road branches off leading to the two observatories of **Las Campanas** (Saturday only at 2pm to book tours tel: 51-207301), and, 30km (18 miles) farther south, ★★ **La Silla** (Saturday 2.30–5.30pm; guided tours which must be booked in advance, tel: 029-463 3000).

On a broad sandy bay by the Pacific, 102km (61 miles) south on Ruta 5, lies ★ **La Serena** (pop. 148,000), the second-oldest town in Chile. It was founded in 1544 to facilitate the sea route to Lima in Peru, the seat of the viceroy and the center of administration at that time. No houses survive from the colonial era, but there are several from the 19th century, when silver and copper mining brought Chile vast wealth. In 1950 President Gabriel González Videla made his birthplace more attractive by having several public buildings erected in the Spanish colonial style. The town experienced a severe earthquake in 1975, after which a great deal of modernization took place.

La Serena beach

In the center the large ★★ **Mercado La Recova** provides everything the region has to offer in two courtyards: ceramic products, textiles, carpets and fruit. The various kinds of papaya are particularly delicious. The ★ **Museo Arqueológico** next door (Monday to Friday 9.30am–5.45pm, Saturday 10am–1pm and 4–7pm, Sunday 10am–1pm) has several fine pre-Spanish exhibits dating from the Molle and Diaguita eras *(see page 54)*. From the center a broad, palm-lined avenue, Avenida Francisco de Aguirre, with its numerous statues, leads down to the sea. At the end of the avenue you'll see the lighthouse that is also the symbol of the town. This marks the start of Avenida del Mar, where you can find hotels and restaurants of almost every price category.

53

Mercado La Recova

The madonna of Andacollo

Valle del Elqui

Excursions from La Serena

The village of ★ **Andacollo** (pop. 10,000) lies 54km (32 miles) southeast of La Serena, and people still come to this region to look for gold.

The village is also a place of pilgrimage: when La Serena was burned by Indians in 1549, legend has it that one of the Spaniards fleeing the blaze took a statue of the Virgin with him and buried it in the sand at Andacollo. Many years later a villager found the statue, and a chapel was built for it. But one day the madonna simply disappeared, and a century later a new one was made by woodcarvers in Peru.

The numerous pilgrims during the 18th century caused a large pilgrimage church to be built, and the madonna became so holy that the clergy in La Serena asked the Pope to crown the mother of God. Leo XIII agreed to the idea, and a golden crown was commissioned from a Parisian goldsmith. On December 26 1901, in a huge new church accommodating 10,000 people, the coronation took place in a grand ceremony.

Ever since, the Fiesta Chica has taken place on the first Sunday in October, when the madonna is dressed in silver. During the Fiesta Grande (December 23–27) she wears gold, and December 26 marks the high-point of the festivities, culminating in a procession carrying the statue through the village.

The Río Elqui reaches the sea near La Serena, and following the river upstream is a delightful experience. The open coastal landscape disappears from view and the bare, dry mountains come ever closer: in the fertile ★★ **Valle del Elqui** there are olive trees, papayas, *chirimoyas* (custard apples), apricots, peaches, and a vast number of grapes. The young vine plants are divided up by tall rows of nets which act as windbreakers.

The village of **El Molle**, famed for its delicious figs and papayas, is 44km (26 miles) farther on. From the first to the ninth centuries this region was the center of the so-called El Molle culture, named after the place where the first artifacts of this period were excavated. The people who forged them were semi-nomadic and made pots, worked metal and tamed domestic animals.

They were followed by the Diaguita Indians, who lived by the rivers in The Small North, or El Norte Chico. Their pottery was mainly reddish-brown, but also black and white with strict geometrical patterns. In the early phase they just made bowls, but later the vessels (which were used for both domestic and ritual purposes) were given handles and began to resemble people and animals in shape. The craftsmanship of the Diaguita became even more sophisticated under the Incas, but these indigenous peoples lost their independence first to the Incas in the late-1400s and then to the Spanish in the mid-1500s.

Farther up the valley, just after the Puclaro Reservoir, is the turn-off to the Cerro Tololo observatory (Saturday, 9am–noon and 1–4pm; to reserve tours, tel: 51-205200).

The town of **Vicuña** (pop. 7,700) lies 66km (39 miles) east of La Serena at an altitude of 610m (2,000ft). The mountains are close by, and the people here enjoy a mild climate and fertile soil. Just outside the town a path leads to the Cerro La Virgen, a small hill with a magnificent view. The vineyards extend a long way up the slopes, and every centimeter of land has been used for agriculture. The area is also notorious for UFO sightings.

North of the plaza is a large ★ **wooden church** dating from 1860, with a painted vault and smooth wooden pillars. Just four blocks east, in Avenida Gabriela Mistral, stands the poet's modest birthplace, with a museum beside it devoted to her work. In 1889 Gabriela Mistral (*see page 82*) was born here as Lucila Godoy Alcayaga, and worked as a teacher in Monte Grande, 30km (18 miles) away in the upper Elqui Valley, where she lies buried in a mausoleum. During her lifetime she received little acclaim from her native land for her melancholy love poetry, and although she was a diplomat for the country; considered eccentric, she lived in Europe, Mexico and the USA.

The village of **Pisco Elqui** lies 2km (1½ mile) to the south of Monte Grande, and the local *pisco* factory here (daily 10am–6pm) is a good place to sample the grape spirit. All around the valley, and particularly in Cochiguaz, 12km (7½ miles) up a valley from Monte Grande, there are a variety of esoteric movements and guru-led communities, offering lodging as well as open-air activities and courses. Some of these are inspired in

Bust of Gabriela Mistral

Vicuña's woooden church

part by the great clarity of the night skies and the sensation that, as the title of a book about this area suggested, *Heaven is Nearer*.

Back to La Serena: from the city center it isn't far along Avenida del Mar to **Coquimbo** (pop. 154,000), which is the capital of this administrative region, on the southern side of the bay, and has most of its houses perched on a hilly peninsula out in the Pacific. This place has had a harbor ever since the Spanish conquest, but it has also been popular with pirates. Sir Francis Drake did some buccaneering here in 1578, for example, and Coquimbo became quite wealthy during the 19th century as an ore shipping center.

The Panamericana highway now hugs the coast southwards for 60km (36 miles), providing good views of the picturesque old resorts in their sheltered bays, as well as of the modern beach paradise of **Las Tacas**. This vacation center even has a heliport to go with its yachting harbor.

In contrast, the elderly wooden houses of ★ **Tongoy** clearly betray their middle-class origins. A white beach – a rarity in this volcanic region – is an attractive place for walks, and the fishermen still catch fish and mend their nets in the various peaceful bays.

Parque Nacional Fray Jorge

Petroglyphs at Valle del Encanto

After roughly 100km (60 miles) there's a turn-off to the **Parque Nacional Fray Jorge** (best visited in the springtime). Above the 500-m (1,650-ft) mark in the Altos de Talinay there's rainforest, with lianas and lichen that are nourished uniquely by fog. This coastal fog, known as *camanchaca*, is formed when warm damp air from the Pacific is cooled down over the land.

Almost 40km (24 miles) east of Ruta 5 is the provincial capital of **Ovalle**, which has a small museum located in the old railway station on the corner of Covarrubias and Antofagasta (Tuesday to Friday 9am–6pm and 3–7pm, weekends and holidays 10am–1pm), containing some fine Diaguita ceramics.

Just 10km (6 miles) beforehand, a rough track branches off southwards into the ★ **Valle del Encanto**, with over 30 petroglyphs *(arte rupestre)* as well as 20 *piedras tacitas*, groups of circular indentations hollowed out of flat rocks in the river bed. These mysterious rock drawings and artifacts have been dated to the El Molle period of around AD700 *(see page 54)*, and the petroglyphs show people with magnificent headdresses, together with stick figures, animals and weird symbols.

The rivers in this region cut deep into the barren mountains. The climate is mild all year round and the summer sun is not as relentlessly hot as it is in The Great North – which is why the rivers reach the coast again, and allow for extensive fruit, vegetable and flower cultivation.

Route 4

Lago Villarrica

Forests, Lakes and Volcanoes

Santiago – Rancagua – Concepción – Temuco – Lago Villarrica – Valdivia – Osorno – Puerto Montt – Chiloé
See map on page 59

Central Chile is like one extended valley streaked with rivers and dotted with towns, villages and hamlets. The snow-covered High Andes lie to the east, and the forested coastal ranges to the west. The Mediterranean climate of the fertile landscape extending as far as 500km (300 miles) south of Santiago produces grapes and citrus fruit. Temuco is the gateway to the enchanted land of lakes and volcanoes, where plumes of smoke often hang above the peaks that are snow-covered even in summer, and the shy puma stalks the forests. This region is distinctive for dairy farming. The good bus and plane networks linking all the major towns, as well as the train service, which reaches as far south as Temuco, make traveling around easy, and allow for some impressive tours through a unique landscape full of contrasts. Make sure you don't miss the pretty little baroque churches on the Isla Grande de Chiloé – with their two-story spires, galleried entrances supported by wooden pillars and shingle roofs, they're artistic gems.

Wooden church on Chiloé

Anyone who feels like doing a lot of sightseeing and is planning to take detours to thermal baths or volcanoes should allow a full 14 days for this route. Chillán, Temuco, Pucón, Valdivia, Osorno or Puerto Montt are all ideal starting points for trips. The forest and lake region south of Temuco takes eight to 10 days to explore properly.

The Valle Central – the long valley that extends south from Santiago to Puerto Montt – is around 1,000km (600 miles)

The crafts market in Chillán

Eaves provide protection

long. Your first stop is **Rancagua** (pop. 207,000), which is capital of this administrative region, a trading center for agricultural produce and close to El Teniente, one of the world's largest underground copper mines. On the road to the mine the route turns off southward after 25km (15 miles) in Coya to the ★ **Termas de Cauquenes** (6km/3½ miles), healthy thermal springs with indoor baths and an open-air swimming pool, where not only the Incas and the Spaniards took the waters but also freedom fighters O'Higgins and San Martín, and even the great naturalist Charles Darwin.

Just before Coya, a turn-off to the north leads to Sewell, the mountain town where miners at El Teniente once lived. Recently restored, Sewell can be visited by prior arrangement with one of the two tour companies appointed by the state copper company for this purpose (tel: 72-210290 or 029-2010992).

The mild and dry climate in the northern part of the long valley favors adobe house construction: projecting eaves covered with clay tiles protect occupants from rain and sun, and make charming galleries when supported by graceful wooden pillars. Even in the small towns you'll often see whole streets of houses in this colonial style.

Follow the Panamericana/Ruta 5 now via San Fernando and Curicó to **Talca** (pop. 194,000). From the northeastern corner of the leafy Plaza de Armas you will arrive at the **Museo O'Higginiano y de Bellas Artes**, Calle 1 Norte (Tuesday to Friday 10am–7pm, Saturday 10.30am–2.30pm, Sunday 2–6pm), which contains a comprehensive collection of art and has rooms typical of the style of 1813–14, when the first junta met here and where Bernardo O'Higgins signed Chile's declaration of independence in 1818.

Cross the Río Maule 18km (10 miles) farther on. It was

at this river in the 15th century that the Mapuches ended the Incas' campaign of conquest.

Formerly located on the site of Chillán Viejo in colonial times, ★ **Chillán** (pop. 148,000) was rebuilt in 1835 after a series of major earthquakes. Then a further very serious quake in 1939 killed 15,000 people and destroyed 90 percent of the town, with the result that hardly any of the buildings here are more than 60 years old. Mexico presented the town with the Escuela México, a school in which allegorical depictions of Chilean and Mexican history by the great Mexican artists Siquieros and Guerrero can be admired in the form of enormous ★ **murals** (Monday to Friday 10am–1pm and 3–6.30pm).

Bernardo O'Higgins

The cathedral in the main square is strikingly contemporary with its 11 semi-elliptical vaulted arches. Make sure you find time to visit Chillán's ★ **crafts market**, where black ceramic figures, bowls and plates from nearby Quinchamalí, and woven goods or hats, make ideal souvenirs.

In Chillán Viejo, in the ★★ **Parque Monumental Bernardo O'Higgins**, the life story of the freedom fighter (1778–1842) is related in mosaics along a 60m (200ft)-long wall. Nearby, on the site of his birthplace, you can visit the **Centro Histórico Cultural** (December to March daily 8am–8pm, April to November 8am– 6.30pm), a country house in the colonial style.

If you then head 82km (49 miles) southeast of Chillán (most of the road is concrete highway here), you'll reach a large skiing and hiking area (1,800m/5,940ft) on the slopes of the ★ **Chillán volcano** (3,122m/10,300ft). The four thermal pools at the spa hotel here are a wonderful way of winding down after a sport-packed day.

The road leading to **Concepción** (pop. 212,000), which, together with adjoining Talcahuano, forms the second-largest city in Chile, crosses the coastal ranges with their numerous rivers. It was in 1550 that Pedro de Valdivia laid the foundation stone for Concepción in the sheltered bay of Penco. In 1751, however, the town was destroyed by an earthquake and seaquake, and rebuilt farther to the south, at the mouth of the Bío Bío River. From 1565 to 1573 Concepción was the political, military and administrative center of the young Spanish kingdom of Chile, but it wasn't until after further devastating earthquakes in 1939 and 1960 that it gained its modern face. The **Pinacoteca**, with the largest collection of Chilean paintings of all epochs anywhere in the country (Tuesday to Friday 10am–6pm,

Saturday 10am–4pm, Sunday 10am–1pm), is of special cultural importance.

Talcahuano (pop. 249,000) is a fishing, forestry and naval port, where since 1950 the country's largest steelworks have been located. The two cities have now merged into one metropolitan mass.

Excursión from Concepción

A good day trip along the coast to the south leads, after 43km/29 miles, to the coal town of **Lota** (pop. 49,000), where you visit what was once the largest mine in the country and follow the miners along a shaft that was opened in 1849. The shafts in the Pique Carlos extend as far as 900m (2,950ft) below sea level.

The lower part of Lota encloses the harbor, while high above the sea on a rocky outcrop there's one of the finest parks in Chile, the ★ **Parque de Lota** (November to March daily 10am–8pm, April to October 10am–6pm), which was laid out in the 19th century by English landscape architects. The wife of Matías Cousiño, the man who founded the mine, looked after it personally, and added numerous fountains, statues and benches.

Continue now, with a view of the thick forests on the Cordillera del Nahelbueta, for another 7km (4 miles) as far as the village of **Laraquete**. Just after you enter it,

Río Laja falls

beyond a small bridge on the left, there's a path along the Las Cruces River. Here you can see a natural rock formation called *piedras cruz*, a variety of andalusite with black cruciform inclusions of carbonaceous matter. This chiastolite is sold in nearly all Chile's jewelry stores.

From Cabrero, back on the Panamericana, it's another 21km (12 miles) to the bridge over the ★ **Río Laja**, just off the highway, where the waters plunge a majestic 20m (65ft) and then force their way through a narrow rocky cleft.

The agricultural town of Los Angeles is a good starting-point for a detour into the varied landscape of the ★★ **Parque Nacional Laguna del Laja**. The second half of the 90km (54 miles) takes you through the steep, narrow valley bordered to the east by a 200m (660ft)-high chunk from the **Antuco volcano** (2,985m/9,850ft), beyond which there is a reservoir. The slopes of the Antuco are popular with skiers in winter, and with anglers and hikers in summer. A 20-km (12-mile) trip across old volcanic ash at the emerald-green Laguna del Laja gives you an unforgettable impression of the magnificent forests against their snowy mountain backdrop.

Bridge across the Malleco

Around 73km (44 miles) to the south of Los Angeles, road and rail bridges cross the ★ **Valle Malleco**. The rail bridge, built in France and shipped to Chile for assembly

in 1890, is one of the most daring iron constructions in the country. After the peace deal with the Mapuches, this rail connection greatly improved the economy of the southern part of the Valle Central.

A few kilometers before Temuco the road branches off eastwards to the ★★ **Parque Nacional Conguillío**, considered to be one of the finest areas of parkland in the country. At its center is the majestic ★ **Llaima volcano** (3,125m/10,310ft). The most active volcano in Chile, it erupted on 22 occasions during the 20th century alone and there's always smoke snaking out of one or other of the two peaks. Over the past 100 years it has created four lakes – Conguillío, Captrén, Arco de Iris and Verde – with melted snow from its summit. Among these you'll see several specimens of the famous 1,000-year old araucaria, or monkey-puzzle tree that can grow to heights of up to 50m (165ft).

Monkey-puzzle trees and the Llaima volcano

Temuco (pop. 233,000), the capital of this administrative region, is also known as Araucanía because it is the center of the Araucanians and the Mapuche Indians. It was not until 1881, after the Indians had been integrated into the state, that Temuco was founded on the site of an old fort. Colonists from Europe were then invited over to till the land, and build up trade and industry. The Araucanía was the bread-basket of Chile, but today the region, now devoted mainly to forest plantations, is one of the poorest in Chile. The ★ **Mercado Central** market hall (Monday to Saturday 8am–8pm, Sunday and public holidays 8.30am–3pm) has a rich selection of wood, textile and ceramic products, and there's always an appetizing aroma from the many snack stands. At the entrance doors, Mapuche women often sell woven carpets with traditional patterns.

Avenida Portales leads east as far as the railroad line. Go two blocks east from here and you'll reach the

Market day in Temuco

Villarrica volcano

Sailing on Lago Villarrica

Valdivia

★★ **Feria**, an open market where the tradespeople are mainly Mapuches, and sell their agricultural produce – from fresh coriander *(cilantro)* to seaweed *(cochayuyo)*. Carlos Thiers' former residence contains the ★★ **Museo Regional de la Araucanía** (Avenida Alemania 084), with folkwear, musical instruments, jewelry and ceramic goods all providing a fascinating impression of Araucanian life. Most Mapuches who have not emigrated to the cities live in traditional communities in the region between Temuco, Cholchol (30km/18 miles northwest), Nueva Imperial in the west and the Río Toltén in the south. There they till their land, keep cattle and sheep, and live in straw-thatched houses. More of these communities are dotted across the landscape as far as Puerto Montt (340km/204 miles farther south).

Southeast of Temuco there's some beautiful landscape on the South Chilean Plate, formed by glacial melt around 10,000 years ago. Several of the snow-capped volcanic cones are right next to the lakes. The ★★ **Lago Villarrica**, at the foot of the volcano of the same name, is one of the most popular lakes in the country. The 24-km (14-mile) long road between Villarrica and Pucón is like one enormous vacation center, with bungalows, hotels and water-sports activities. **Villarrica** (pop. 31,000) was founded in 1551 before being destroyed soon afterwards by the Mapuches. Around a century ago it was rebuilt, and today lives off forestry and agriculture as well as tourism.

Since 1934, when its Gran Hotel was built, ★ **Pucón** has developed from a simple cattle-market town to the most famous vacation center in southern Chile, complete with casino.

The mild summer climate is especially favorable for trekking, hiking, fishing, riding, golf and rafting; and you can even take a short trip by plane to admire the crater of the Villarrica volcano (2,840m/ 9,372ft). In winter the slopes of the still-smoking volcano, which had 10 powerful eruptions during the 20th century alone, are very popular with skiers. Climbing it has to be done with a guide and you need to be fit as well as well-equipped (the organizers provide everything) for the six to eight hours it takes to ascend and descend through the snow and ice. It's well worth the exertion, though, for the view at the summit down inside the glowing center of the mountain, and across the fascinating landscape surrounding it.

★ **Valdivia** (pop. 130,000), in the middle of undulating landscape, was the most important harbor town on the south coast before the construction of the Panama Canal. During the 17th century, to protect it from frequent pirate raids and Mapuche attack, the forts of Corral, Niebla and

Mancera were built on the broad estuary of the Río Valdivia (18km/11 miles from the town center). Valdivia suffered a catastrophe in 1960: the tidal wave from an undersea earthquake destroyed vast parts of it, flinging large ships and whole buildings far inland. Three days later the massive wave reached Japan. New Valdivia has now appeared on the Calle Calle and Valdivia rivers like a phoenix from the ashes.

A day trip round Valdivia could start at the bridge over the Calle Calle, where the fortified tower of Torreón del Barro (1781) stands. From there, Avenida Picarte leads straight through the center to the western side of the bend in the river. Near the ★ **Mercado Fluvial**, where magnificent fruit, vegetables and fish can be bought on boats, the excursion ships leave for the restored fortresses of **Niebla**, ★ **Corral** and **Mancera**. A broad bridge connects the mainland with the Isla Teja, between the Calle Calle, Cruces and Valdivia rivers. In its northeastern corner are the Universidad Austral, the ★ **Botanical Garden** with its native flora, and the Parque Saval.

Corral Fortress and the Botanical Garden

Valdivia celebrates its foundation by the Spanish *conquistador* Pedro de Valdivia (1552) in February each year with shows and folklore: on the third Saturday in the month, during the ★ **Noche Valdiviana**, decorated boats, accompanied by floating lanterns and firework displays, float down the Calle Calle at dusk.

A good day-long excursion from Valdivia is to ★ **Lago Ranco**, which has been barely touched by tourism, and then back to the Panamericana. Travel to **Futrono**, 42km (25 miles) from Reumén. Soon the snow-covered volcanoes of Puyehue, Casablanca, Puntiagudo, Osorno and Calbuco will come into view, along with the deep-blue lake. A great way to experience the full beauty of Lago Ranco is to travel clockwise round it as far as the town

Lago Ranco

of the same name. A Mapuche reserve is located in the middle of the lake.

The town of **Osorno** (pop. 132,000) was one of the centers of German immigration that began in 1852. Three hard-working generations turned forest into fertile arable land, gave the landscape its present appearance and soon turned Osorno into southern Chile's leading agricultural center. The Catedral San Mateo in the main square, with its filigree belfry, was rebuilt after the earthquake of 1960. One block south, in Avenida Bilbao, exhibits from pre-Spanish times can be seen in the ★ **Museo Municipal** (Monday to Friday 10am–12.30pm and 2.30–6pm).

A good day trip from Osorno is to take the road, lined with fields and meadows, to peaceful and uncrowded ★ **Lago Puyehue**, 45km (27 miles) from Osorno.

Colonial heritage in Frutillar

Osorno dominates the landscape

The next stop on the route is **Lago Llanquihue**. The first German to come to the southern part of the Valle Central was the botanist Bernhard Philippi in 1842, who persuaded hundreds of settlers to found the towns of Puerto Varas, Llanquihue, Frutillar and Puerto Octay.

In ★ **Frutillar** (pop. 9,000) there are still several old houses dating from these colonial times, but the upper town only really started to develop once the railroad came here in 1907. There's an interesting **Museo Colonial Alemán** (daily 10am–2pm and 3–6pm) documenting the town's German origins; and halfway between Frutillar and Llanquihue, the **Monumento a los Antepasados** (1937) commemorates the first German settlers, with 80 names engraved in bronze.

Travel through the small town of Llanquihue and on to **Puerto Varas**. The wooden church of Sagrado Corazón de Jesús is very attractive; its German architect based the design on a church in the Black Forest.

On the way to Ensenada there are numerous fine beaches, hotels and restaurants, and (after 21km/13 miles) the ★ **Watermill** open-air museum, which also serves good food.

Many salmon farms have been established on the west and south banks of the Lago Llanquihue as well as in the Gulf of Reloncaví (south of Puerto Montt) and are now the area's most important economic activity.

The landscape around the lake is dominated by the perfectly shaped cone of the **Osorno volcano** (2,952m/9,740ft), the last eruption of which was described in detail by Charles Darwin. Since then the crater has been enveloped by a thick layer of snow and ice. Tours to the summit (for experienced, fit climbers only) are available with a guide from travel companies in Puerto Varas and Puerto Montt.

The pleasant harbor town of **Ensenada** is a good starting point for a ★★ **trip through the Andes**, beginning at the ★★ **Parque Nacional Vicente Pérez Rosales**. The first stop on the way is the waterfall of the ★ **Río Petrohué**, from which several hiking routes fan out into some magnificent forest. The ship-and-bus trip through this mountain region is a fascinating experience. It starts at Petrohué on the western shore of ★★ **Lago Todos Los Santos** (All Saints' Lake), from where you travel by hydrofoil across the water, past massive rocks and forests all around, as far as Peulla, reached 90 minutes later. Passengers are served lunch in the hotel of the same name before taking a 26-km (16-mile) bus trip through the ever-narrowing mountain landscape as far as Puerto Frías (in Argentina), and then a 20-minute voyage by ship across Lago Frías. The last 3km (2 miles) overland as far as the **Lago Nahuel Huapi** pass through a thick forest of 1,000-year-old alerce trees (Patagonian cypresses), which grow to a height of 45m (150ft) or more. Then a further hydrofoil takes you to San Carlos de Bariloche in Argentina.

Petrohué falls

The city of ★ **Puerto Montt** (pop. 156,000), capital of this administrative region, lies in a broad bay next to the sea. It is protected from the cold southwest wind by the hills on the Isla Tenglo. The locals travel out to this island to eat the traditional meat and shellfish casserole *curanto (see page 86)*. In the east the landscape is dominated by the Calbuco volcano (2,015m/6,650ft), the summit of which blew apart during an eruption in the 19th century.

On the western edge of Puerto Montt in ★★ **Angelmó**, the former trading center of the Chiloé inhabitants has turned into a picturesque open-air fish and crafts market, where textiles, copper goods, woodcarvings and dried seafood on strings are on sale in colorful rows of stores. The restaurants all use ingredients that are guaranteed to be fresh.

Couple in Puerto Montt

Lago Todos Los Santos

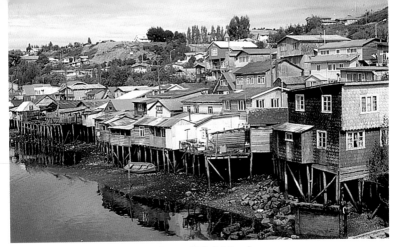

Pile-dwellings in Castro

Rural idyll

Cathedral interior

Green Chiloé Island

The Ice Age glaciers left powerful traces in the mountains of southern South America, and many of the deep valleys formed were flooded by the steadily rising seawater. This is how the myriad tiny islands, the Patagonian fjord landscape and Chiloé Island came into being. The latter is 180km (108 miles) long, and has impenetrable forest in its western section and broad hills and valleys in the east, where the fishermen and farmers live – many to 100 and older. There's a ferry connection to Chiloé Island every 10 minutes from Pargua (45km/27 miles west of Puerto Montt).

The northernmost town is **Ancud** (pop. 27,000) with Fort San Antonio, built in 1770 to protect the harbor. In 1567 the capital ★ **Castro** was founded; located 88km (52 miles) south, it was soon settled by Franciscan monks. The ★ **Catedral de San Francisco de Castro** was built from local hardwood in 1910, and is remarkable for the attractive grain of its wood, as well as the height of its interior. On the northern bay, the locals live in ★ **pile-dwellings**, known as *palafitos* – some of them brightly colored – to cope with the 7-m (23-ft) difference in water level each time the tides come in. The **Mirador Cerro Huaihuén** (a look-out point) affords breathtaking views over the city and across the Chacao Channel toward the mainland.

In 1607 Jesuits settled on the island and worked as missionaries from here to the southern tip of the continent, as far as the Magellan Straits. Each community had to build a church in which a mission visit took place once a year. For this reason there are still 160 lovingly decorated wooden churches on this island, dating from the 17th and 18th centuries. The ★★ **churches** of Tenaún, Dalcahue, Achao, Nercón, Chonchi, Quinchao and Vilupulli are prized for their unique architectural beauty and form part of UNESCO's World Heritage List.

Route 5

Fjords, Glaciers and Remoteness

Northern Patagonia: Carretera Austral – Puerto Montt – Chaitén – Puyuhuapi – Coihaique
Southern Patagonia: Punta Arenas – Puerto Natales – Torres del Paine – Tierra del Fuego *Map on page 70*

Impenetrable forests, glaciers, fjords, lakes, endless pampas, condors, guanacos (a relative of the domesticated llama), ñandu ostriches, penguins and a great deal of remoteness are the distinctive features of Patagonia, which extends for 2,300km (1,400 miles) from Puerto Montt to the Magellan Straits. The mountainous and forested north is crossed by a wild and romantic rough track which at present ends up at a lake near Villa O'Higgins. South of the mighty 350km (210 mile)-long ice cap of the Southern Ice Field, which has to be bypassed along Argentine roads, are the bizarre-shaped Torres del Paine. The beauty of the mountains and glaciers of Tierra del Fuego can best be appreciated from the deck of a ship.

Family gathering

67

Overland tours can be undertaken only with a sturdy four-wheel-drive vehicle. Accommodations are available in all the larger towns, but have to be booked a long time in advance if you're planning to be here in January or February. There's a 10-day tour for Northern Patagonia alone, starting at Chiloé (see page 66), where you have to take the car ferry (22 hours) from Chonchi to Puerto Chacabuco/Aisén. From there you'll have an adventurous three to four days as far as Villa O'Higgins and then back to Coihaique. Traveling on further to Puerto Montt takes around three more days but is more than worth it for the magnificent landscape.

If you feel like going by car to Punta Arenas, take the Carretera Austral from Puerto Montt to Chile Chico (three and a half days minus excursions). The trip through the Argentine pampas as far as Calafate lasts one day, though it's certainly worth taking several days' break in the Parque Nacional Los Glaciares (with Lago Viedma and Lago Argentino). Taking this route you'll arrive at the spellbinding Parque Nacional Torres del Paine from the north. A partly rough and partly concreted track, with plenty of varied scenery, connects the Torres with Punta Arenas.

Another possibility (described in this chapter) is to fly from Puerto Montt to Punta Arenas and then explore the sights of Southern Patagonia by car from there (which takes three to four days).

ROUTE 5
Northern Patagonia

0   100 km

N

Patagonian fjord (above) and the Carretera Austral

San Rafael Glacier

Northern Patagonia

The opening of the ★★ **Carretera Austral** in 1988 provided Northern Patagonia with access to modern Chile. Charles Darwin referred to this region, where very few Indians lived, as the 'green desert'. Settlement gradually began from the coasts in the second half of the 19th century. In 1937 a law was passed allowing the trees to be burned down to provide grazing land. This destroyed the natural forest, the charcoal remains of which can still be seen here and there, and in some regions not a single one of the magnificent trees was left standing. Since the 1970s, very expensive reforestation programs have been trying to repair at least some of the damage.

On the 200-km (120-mile) trip from Puerto Montt to **Chaitén** (pop. 4,000) you'll need to take ferries three times to cross fjords. These ferries (which operate till midnight, but sometimes with long waiting times) don't have fixed schedules, but sail whenever necessary.

As far as **Puerto Puyuhuapi**, 199km (119 miles) farther on, the route is spectacular, traveling uphill through thick forest, past beautiful blue lakes, hanging glaciers and emerald-green rivers.

The ★★ **Termas de Puyuhuapi**, 7km (4 miles) to the south, can be reached by boat (10am, 12.30pm, 7pm and on request). These three enormous thermal pools on the edge of a fjord, surrounded by giant ferns and bamboo, are a great place to revive yourself, not least because the pools are 39°C (103°F) and the sea 12°C (54°F). Then you can relax in the hotel *(see page 102)*, which is very expensive but located in a beautiful spot between the forest and the water.

The hotel also organizes day trips in its own catamaran to the fjords and also the ★★ **San Rafael Glacier** (tel: 2-225 6489 to make bookings). This is a truly breathtaking experience, as the boat goes right up to the edge of the ice sheet, often accompanied by dolphins and great crested grebes.

On the way to the next point on the journey, Coihaique, it's worth taking a detour after 13km (8 miles) to the ★ **Parque Nacional Queulat** and then walking to the Ventisquero Colgante (Hanging Glacier) through the wild landscape. On the way you'll cross an old-style rope bridge across a thundering river: with a roar, the sections of glacier fall hundreds of meters into the sea.

After 357km (220 miles) the road forks and ends in the west at the little town of **Puerto Aisén** with its harbor of Puerto Chacabuco (another 49km/29 miles). There are boat trips from here to the San Rafael Glacier *(see opposite)*.

Coihaique locals and their surroundings

The town of ★ **Coihaique** (pop. 45,000) is 420km (252 miles) from Chaitén. The capital of this administrative region, it's a perfect base from which to explore the area. To the east, among rough rocks, there are the three lakes of Cástor, Pólux and Frío; the trip westwards starts on the bridge over the Simpson River with a view of the Piedra del Indo rock, so named because of its similarity to an Indian's profile; Lago Atravesado and Lago Elizalde are out in the broad pampas; and the eastern side of the Andes has a dry climate and only 500mm (20in) of rain a year. Devastating forest clearance has wrought immeasurable damage in this region.

After the airport of Balmaceda the landscape becomes forested and mountainous again. The steep peaks of the Cerro Castillo (2,657m/8,770ft) dominate the scenery. Shortly before the village of the same name, 713km (428 miles) into the trip, the road branches off southeastwards to the largest lake in the country, the **Lago General Carrera** (which on the Argentine side is called Lago Buenos Aires). The small inland harbor of Puerto Ibañez is very important for the agricultural and forestry trades. A car/passenger ferry brings tourists to the southern bank of the lake, to **Chile Chico**, a village-like center of fruit and vegetable cultivation.

The track that runs westward along the lake for 125km (75 miles) meets up in El Maitén with the Carretera Austral from the north (169km/101 miles). On the way you can see the effects of the Mount Hudson (2,615m/8,630ft) volcanic eruption in 1991: the ash it produced buried animals, trees and grazing land all the way to Argentina.

Another 67km (40 miles) farther on you'll reach the village of Cochrane (pop. 2,200), and a further 123km (74 miles) after that, the harbor of **Puerto Yungay**. Here the Pacific waterways connect the glaciers of the Campo de Hielo Norte (Northern Ice Field) with those of the 350km (210 mile)-long Campo de Hielo Sur (Southern Ice Field). The ice masses of the latter block the route farther south,

Fuerte Bulnes

and the road reaches only as far as Villa O'Higgins. Of the roughly 1,200km (745 miles) of the Carretera Austral between Puerto Montt and Villa O'Higgins, the southernmost section from Villa Cerro Castillo is considered the most exhilarating and adventurous. The grandiose scenery, where rivers have cut deep into the earth and are framed by steep mountains and impenetrable rainforest, is perpetually stunning.

Southern Patagonia

In 1848, ★ **Punta Arenas** (pop. 116,000), the capital of this administrative region, was successfully established. Five years previously an attempt to do the same thing 58km (35 miles) south, at ★ **Fuerte Bulnes**, had failed. The pioneer village, fortress-like with its wooden palisade, has been reconstructed, and the trip there takes about half a day. The road skirts the Magellan Straits and provides fine views of Tierra del Fuego and the snow-clad mountains of the southern islands. Just before Fuerte Bulnes, at the 51-km (32-mile) mark, a **monolith** marks the center of Chile: from

ROUTE 5
Southern Patagonia and
Tierra del Fuego

0   100 km

this point Arica and the South Pole, where Chile's land rights end, are each 5,160km (4,000 miles) away.

Punta Arenas

The first attempt to found a Spanish settlement in the area was made as long ago as 1584, at **Puerto de Hambre** (Hunger Harbor), 2km (1 mile) away. The unfortunate settlers died of hunger after their supply route had been cut off for more than three years, or were killed by the Indian Alacalufe tribe. Their bodies were discovered in 1587 by the English pirate Thomas Cavendish, who gave the place its name.

71

Punta Arenas experienced an economic boom towards the end of the 19th century as a trading center. Around the same time the shepherd dynasty of the Estancieros also grew rich, and this left its mark on the city's appearance. But when oil was discovered on Tierra del Fuego in 1945, the town became even more important.

A walk through Punta Arenas should start in the main square, the **Plaza Muñoz Gamero**. Between Magellan cypresses you can see the statue of the Portuguese navigator Ferdinand Magellan, surrounded by four Indians, looking across the straits that bear his name. Since they were discovered in 1520, many ships have no longer needed to round the feared Cape Horn.

Statue of Magellan

Several of the townhouses around Plaza Muñoz belonged to the sheep-herding families. In 1876 there were just 300 sheep, but 10 years later the figure had risen to 150,000, and soon it was up in the millions. The ★ **Museo Regional de Magallanes**, formerly the Palacio Braun Menéndez (summer: Monday to Saturday 10.30am–5pm, Sunday, 10.30am–2pm; winter: daily 10.30am–2pm), is a fine example of the lavish lifestyle the rich once enjoyed here.

The ★ **Palacio Sara Braun de Nogueira** is used partly by the Club de la Unión Chilean gentleman's club and partly as a hotel. The ★ **Museo Regional Salesiano**, next to the church in Avenida M Bulnes (Tuesday to Sunday

Hunters in the Museo Regional Salesiano

El Indio Desconocido

10am–noon and 3–6pm during summer, 10am–1pm and 2.30–6pm in winter), provides a good insight into the life of the aboriginal population and the nature of the region.

Two blocks farther on, in the ★★ **Cementerio** (daily daylight hours), visit the magnificent mausoleums of the town's famous families and the Unknown Indian, El Indio Desconocido. This bronze statue was erected in honor of the Ona Indians, who lived on Tierra del Fuego, and is always decorated and thought to work miracles. The main gate was financed by Sara Braun, last survivor of the powerful local family; she was the only person allowed through it, and it remains closed to this day.

Outside the town, in Avenida Bulnes, you can see **El Ovejero**, the popular monument to shepherds. Also worthy of note in the same street, but farther north, is the ★ **Instituto de la Patagonia** (winter: Monday to Friday 8.30am–noon and 2.30–4pm, Saturday 8.30am–noon; summer: also Sunday 8.30am–noon and until 6pm on weekdays) with an interesting library and open-air museum, and artifacts from the time of the town's foundation.

An excursion by plane or cruise ship from Punta Arenas to the ★ **Beagle Channel**, a strait between mountains, forest and lonely islands, will introduce you to the land of the Yamanes, nomadic Indians who lived by fishing. The first whites discovered this region on *The Beagle* in 1830, which had Charles Darwin on board. The captain of the ship, Fitzroy, took Yamanes to England to educate them for two years, but back in their homeland they reverted to their normal way of life. When an English mission later started activities in the Yamanes' region, they were attacked by the very Indians who had been 'civilized'.

Trip to the Torres del Paine

Off the coast, on the trip northward along the **Magellan Strait**, you can see **Magdalena** and **Marta Island**, where there are huge colonies of penguins (excursions are available from Punta Arenas).

On Ruta 9 there's a turn-off after 27km (16 miles) toward **Seno Otway**. After the large Pecket coal pit is an 80-hectare (200-acre) nesting site for Magellan penguins *(Spheiscus magellanicus)*, who breed and rear their young here between October and March.

On the 254-km (152-mile) asphalt road through the pampas you'll see ñandus and flamingos. Ñandus are small members of the ostrich family, once hunted for their fine feathers but today, like the flamingos who breed in the steppe lagoons, they are protected. In the small town of **Puerto Natales**, where numerous cruise ships dock, lookout for cormorants and black-necked swans.

An unforgettable day trip by boat westwards goes to ★ **Last Hope Fjord** (Ultima Esperanza), where the high-

Cueva del Milodón

point of the journey is the calving **Serrano Glacier**.

A half-day trip can also be made to the ★ **Cueva del Milodón** cave (25km/15 miles northwest). The buffalo-sized giant sloth called the *milodón* died out in the Pleistocene era. But parts of its fur and skeleton discovered here (and now in London) enabled a reconstruction of the animal to be made, which can be seen in the cave.

On the way north, and especially in January during the sheep-shearing season, it's worthwhile stopping in the village of **Cerro Castillo**, originally a small sheep farm founded in 1906. There's a small hotel here now.

The highlight of this trip, however, are the stunning ★★★ **Torres del Paine** (44km/26 miles along a rough track from Puerto Natales). It took 12 million years for the mountain to push its way out of the ice, and as the Ice Age ended it left a bizarre formation of granite towers and horns as well as emerald-green and turquoise lakes. Playful guanacos, shy ñandus, black-necked swans, gray foxes and condors soaring in the sky are all here to admire.

The park has a relatively mild microclimate all year round: in the east this is thanks to the steppe-like vegetation of the dry grassland, and in the west it is protected from the storms of the Pacific. In August the beech trees turn a beautiful golden color. UNESCO declared this national park a biosphere reserve in 1978. Your visit to the park should include at least one overnight stay, but remember that the weather is not that stable. The athletically inclined can go hiking, riding, rafting and trekking.

A trip from the Laguna Amarga to the Hostería Lago Grey leads from east to west along the mighty rocks, past turquoise lakes, and over the gently rounded rocks and hills. The slate-covered peaks keep changing appearance in the light, and the landscape is incredibly restful.

Beagle Channel

73

Torres del Paine

Lonely Cape Horn

Porvenir church

Puerto Williams

Tierra del Fuego

The largest island in South America is as delightful as it is forbidding. Before the last Ice Age it was connected by land to the continent across the Magellan Strait, but today the waters of the Atlantic and the Pacific merge here. The broad expanses in the north and east contrast with a bizarre, inhospitable mountain landscape in the southwest. To add to the rather gloomy atmosphere, the westernmost island is called Desolación (Desolation).

The island's climate is not as harsh as you might expect for its location, although the weather is renowned for being erratic. The best time to visit is during the summer months, from November to March, when daylight lasts for up to 20 hours.

The explorer Ferdinand Magellan told Charles V that he had seen columns of smoke rising from the large island in 1520, and dubbed it the Land of Smoke. But the Spanish king decided to give it the more poetic name Tierra del Fuego, Land of Fire.

The smoke actually came from the fires of the Ona tribe, who had lived there as guanaco hunters for the previous 10,000 years. But shortly after the first foreign incursion in 1879 there were great changes on the island. The state took vast tracts of land for sheep farming, thereby driving the Indians out. The latter soon adapted, however – a sheep was far easier to catch than a guanaco – and the Ona were hunted as thieves and very cruelly persecuted. Even though an Anglican mission did its best to save them, the tribe gradually died out.

The best place to start an automobile tour of Tierra del Fuego is **Porvenir** (pop. 4,700), the capital of the province. The **Museo Provincial** (Monday to Thursday 9am–5pm, Friday 9am–4pm, weekends 10am–1.30pm and 3–5pm) on the main plaza documents the history of this remote region very well, with mummies, stuffed indigenous animals and memorabilia of one of the island's leaders, Julio Popper.

On the way to **Lago Blanco**, roughly 240km (144 miles) from Porvenir, you'll pass several sheep farms with old manor houses. The south is covered with increasingly dense forests. Near the lake many colonies of beavers, originally imported from Canada for the fur trade, have built dams and efforts are now being made to control their numbers.

In **Puerto Williams** on the north coast of Isla Navarino, the **Museo Martín Gusinde** (October to March Monday to Thursday 9am–7.15pm, weekends 2.30–6.30pm; April to September Monday to Thursday 9am–1pm and 2.30–6pm, Saturday 2.30–6.30pm) provides information about the aboriginal inhabitants of the southernmost tip of the earth. The German priest for whom the museum is named lived with the Qawasqar, Yamanes and Ona tribes from 1918 to 1924.

Route 6

Stone giants on Rapa Nui

All Alone in the Pacific

Isla Robinson Crusoe and Easter Island (Rapa Nui)
See maps on page 76

75

Among the small islands of the Juan Fernández Archipelago, 650km (390 miles) west of Valparaíso in the Pacific, the one most likely to enchant nature lovers will definitely be the Isla Robinson Crusoe, with its subtropical vegetation.

A further 3,000km (1,800 miles) in the direction of Tahiti is the solitary volcanic island of Rapa Nui, also known as Easter Island. Stone giants watch over this outpost of Polynesia, and for years now the *moai*, as they are called, have captured the imagination of tourists and explorers alike with their mystical aura.

The Juan Fernández Archipelago consists of three islands: Alexander Selkirk, Santa Clara and the largest, Robinson Crusoe, reached by a 2½ hour flight from Santiago. Lan Chile operates four flights to and from Easter Island each week.

Isla Robinson Crusoe

In 1574 the Portuguese Juan Fernandez came ashore on this partly rough and rocky island, and discovered nothing but thick forests and colonies of sea-lions; the latter are still here today, frolicking in the bays.

The archipelago was formed by volcanic eruptions millions of years ago on the Nazca Plate, and it wanders several centimeters every year toward the coast of South America. The islands were visited by pirates during the 17th and 18th centuries, among them the Scot Alexander Selkirk, who was left here, on his own request, in 1704,

...and miniature ones too

Isla Robinson Crusoe

Footprint in the sand

and survived living off the land until he was rescued four years later. The novel *Robinson Crusoe* by Daniel Defoe was based on his experiences.

Since the archipelago lies outside the chill Humboldt sea current, large parts of the mountainous landscape are covered with subtropical vegetation. Ferns the size of trees and numerous rare plants cover the rocks just as they have for millions of years. Isla Robinson Crusoe, declared a biosphere reserve by UNESCO in 1977, is the only place in the world where the red hummingbird can be found. The 600 islanders live in San Juan Bautista on Cumberland Bay, earning money from tourism and fishing for lobsters. An attractive forest track leads 3km (1½ miles) westward from San Juan Bautista to the Mirador Selkirk observation point, where the lonely Scot kept a lookout.

Easter Island – Rapa Nui

Around 2.5 million years ago, a massive volcanic eruption produced the eastern corner of ★★★ **Easter Island** (Rapa Nui, or Isla de Pascua in Spanish), the Poike. The southern part, Ranu Kau, was formed a million years ago, and around 240,000 years ago came the Maunga Terevaka (507m/1,670ft), the highest mountain on the island. The island is 180 sq km (112 sq miles), and its population of 3,800 lives (mainly off tourism) in Hanga Roa, the only town. Maize, beans and bananas are also grown.

The first settlers came here from Polynesia in the fifth century – a culture distinctive for its enormous stone statues *(moai)*. The peoples were referred to as 'the long-eared ones' because of their custom of using stakes to extend their ear lobes as far as their shoulders. In the 14th century another Polynesian culture arrived on the island in the shape of the so-called 'bird people', led by their chieftain Hotu Matu'a. At the end of the 17th century there was a civil war, brought on by the tensions caused by a rise in the population to 15,000, in the course of which the 'bird people' annihilated the 'long ears'.

Each clan of the long-eared people had a cult site to look after, called an *ahu*. If a chieftain felt that death was imminent, he had a *moai* created from the tuff of the

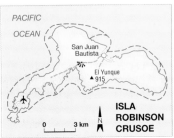

ISLA ROBINSON CRUSOE

PACIFIC OCEAN

San Juan Bautista

El Yunque ▲ 915

0 3 km N

EASTER ISLAND

PACIFIC OCEAN

Maunga Terevaka ▲ 509   Anakena   Hekii

Tepeu

Akivi

Tahai

Hanga-Roa

Orongo   Vinapu

Ranu Kau

Ranu Raraku

Peninsula ▲ Poike   Puakatiki

0 5 km N

Ranu Raraku volcano, and it was placed on the *ahu* after his death, facing his tribe. That way he felt that his strength, wisdom and protection could be transferred to his grave in the *ahu*. Many of the impressive platforms with the *moai* – which can be up to 20m (66ft) high and weigh several tons – have been restored. These include Tahai, Vinapu, Akivi, Hekii and Amakena, where Hotu Matu'a landed.

The Ranu Kau and the Bird Man

In Orongo, a place on the edge of the Ranu Kau volcano where the first settlers worshiped the creator god Makemake, the island's 'bird man' was chosen each year. For this to happen, the first sea-swallow's egg had to be brought from the island of Moto Nui, around 1km (⅔mile) away; believed to be an incarnation of Makemake, it was treated with extreme care. Young men from each tribe then had a swimming contest, and the chieftain of the tribe that won was accorded the status of 'bird man', or *Tangata Manu*, which also involved several ceremonial duties. The bird was the symbol of divinity, and reliefs of the bird men were engraved in the rocks near Orongo.

The inhabitants of Rapa Nui used a system of symbols which has not yet been completely deciphered. The letters were cut into small wooden strips *(rongo rongo)*. The islanders were also excellent sculptors, and remain so to this day. Just take a look inside the small ★ **church** in Hanga Roa, where the mixture of Christianity and local religion is evident: the saints have birds' heads.

Cemetery at Hanga Roa

When the Dutch admiral Jacob Roggeveen became the first European to set foot on the island in 1722, it marked the start of a tragic development: parts of the population were sent to the Guano Islands of Peru as slaves, and others emigrated, so that by 1877 there were only 111 inhabitants left. Chile decided to support them, and annexed the island – which until then had been 'stateless' – in the year 1888.

Art and Architecture

Architecture

From the simple clay-brick villages of colonial Chile, through the ornate Parisian facades of 19th-century Santiago, to the hi-tech glass-faced office blocks of its cities today, Chile's architecture is testament to the country's multicultural history and influences.

In the pre-Spanish period there were no great architects at work here on the scale of those in, say, Bolivia or Peru. The remains of some old fortresses can be found in the north, but it was only in the 17th century that single-aisled churches were built in the remote settlements there. They reveal a mixture of Spanish baroque and Andean elements: outwardly simple and massive, with statues of popular saints on the inside, and with a clear separation between the main body of the church and its tower – symbolical of the male and female forms.

The old colonial villages were built from adobe bricks, a mixture of clay and straw pressed together into blocks and then left to dry in the sun. These and a large number of the wooden and stone structures dating from colonial times have been destroyed by earthquakes over the years. But the elegant neoclassical style, with its pillared facades, which appeared in the coastal towns during the 19th century, is still very much in evidence at Iquique (see page 42–3). Chile's prosperity at the end of the 19th century changed the face of Santiago, making it very French in style. For rich Chileans at that time, Paris was the epitome of elegance, their secret capital.

Few countries have as mismatched a range of architectural styles as Chile. Flat adobe-brick houses preponderate in the rural areas; their veranda roofs supported by narrow wooden pillars help keep the rooms and galleries cool. In the south the houses are built mainly of wood, because it is very flexible in earthquakes and plentiful in supply. Wherever German immigrants colonized the country (as in Valdivia, see page 62–3) there are large estate houses that could have been transported straight from Germany, except that they are entirely of wood. On the Chiloé archipelago (see page 66) the architectural highlights are beautiful wooden churches, all the more striking because they often stand starkly alone on a headland; built by Jesuits in the 17th century, they feature fine shingles, with pillared porticoes to support the multi-story tower, and the center of the interior is spanned by an artistic wooden vault.

In the towns of modern Chile earthquake-proof *torres* (towers) and monumental skyscrapers – still made of concrete or brick a few years back, but now increasingly glass-faced, particularly in the business districts of eastern Santiago – reflect the country's present prosperity.

Neoclassical elegance in Iquique

Door detail on Chiloé

Art

Before the turn of the 20th century, Chile scarcely featured on the artistic world map. What little painting originated from the country was highly derivative of European works. But Chilean painters set off on their own path with the appearance of the Impressionist Juan Francisco González (1853–1933). His pictures no longer reflected the academic severity of his forerunners' works, but emphasized the freedom of nature. Pablo Burchard (1875–1964) followed in his footsteps by immortalizing apparently uninteresting objects such as lonely trees in the center of landscapes, or walls in village streets.

After these painters came the so-called Generación del 13, whose exponents, such as Ezequiel Plaza and Arturo Gordon, focused on the castigation of big-city life.

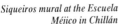

Mural at Museo a Cielo Abierto in Valparaíso, erstwhile haunt of Roberto Matta and others

More recently, the most noted painter to come out of Chile is the Surrealist Roberto Matta (1911–2002). He has been dubbed the first *Star Wars* artist and science-fiction artist because his canvases depict cosmic spaces in which Surrealist mythological creatures do battle with the forces of chaos. Matta's paintings hang in many of the world's great museums.

Also of note are the works of Nemesio Antúnez (1918–93), Mario Carreño (born in Cuba in 1913 and died in Santiago in 1999), both of whom created Surrealist renditions of everyday items, and Mario Toral (born in 1934).

In contrast, some of the most striking and original art in Chile is the allegorical murals of events in Chilean and Mexican history, by the Mexican artists David Alfaro Siqueiros and Xavier Guerrero in Chillán *(see page 59)*.

As for sculpture, the powerful *Roots of America* of Samuel Román (1907–90), the totem-like wood or stone monuments of Marta Colvin (1907–95), and *Tree Man* by Osvaldo Peña (born 1950) are among Chile's finest works.

Siqueiros mural at the Escuela Méjico in Chillán

Theater, Music and Film

Theater

Theater is a lively feature of the cultural scene in Chile. Actor and director Andrés Pérez ran the Gran Circo Teatro group until his death in 2002, putting on magical performances of works such as *La Negra Ester*, based on a poem by Roberto Parra, or *Popol Vuh*, a Maya legend about the birth of humanity.

The theater at the Catholic University in Santiago puts on both classical and modern performances, as well as children's theater. Many small ensembles delight audiences with their imagination and inventiveness.

Music

Several performers have achieved world renown, especially the pianist Claudio Arrau and the tenor Ramón Vinay, whose importance is still undisputed even after his death. Other pianists famed far beyond the borders of Chile are Rosita Renard, Flora Guerra, Alfredo Perl, Alfonso Montecino and Oscar Gacitúa, as well as Roberto Bravo with his popular piano arrangements of Latin-American music.

81

Musical life in Santiago revolves around four permanent orchestras, including a youth orchestra that was set up by the former president Patricio Aylwin.

At the beginning of the 1960s the singers Violeta Parra, Victor Jara and Patricio Manns started collecting and performing folk tunes and songs from the country's original inhabitants and rural population. Soon these songs changed from pure folklore to take on a heavy political and satirical bent. It was the very popular Violeta Parra who wrote the song *Gracias a la Vida (Thanks to Life)*, made world-famous by Joan Baez.

Violeta Parra

Film

Quality film and television productions have been increasing since the end of the dictatorship in 1990. The country's best-known current film-makers include: Silvio Caiozzi, who portrayed the conflict between the generations in a Valparaíso family in *La Luna en el Espejo (The Moon in the Mirror)*, in which actress Gloria Münchmeyer played the lead role and received an award at Venice Biennale in 1991; Miguel Littín, who told the story of Latin America in his *El Chacal de Nahueltoro (The Jackal of Nahueltoro)*; Gustavo Graaef-Merino, whose crime movie *Johny Cien Pesos (Johnny 100 Pesos*, 1993) was based on a true story of a hold-up in Santiago; and Andrés Wood, whose film *Machuca* about the social divisions that underpinned the Pinochet dictatorship received international recognition.

Literature

Chile's early literary works were primarily descriptions of the country and its inhabitants. The most important in the early years of Hispano America was by Alonso de Ercilla y Zúñiga (1533–94), the former page of Philip II, who arrived on Chilean soil in 1557 as a warrior but soon achieved great fame with his 37-song epic *La Araucana.* In 1644 the Chilean Jesuit priest Alonso de Ovalle published his *Histórica Relación del Reyno de Chile (Historical Description of the Kingdom of Chile).*

Gabriela Mistral

But it was not until the post-colonial period that Chilean literature properly began. Alberto Blest Gana (1831–1920), an officer and a diplomat, achieved literary fame within the country for novels such as *Martín Rivas* (1862). Influenced by Honoré de Balzac, it is among the classics of Chilean literature today.

In 1889 Gabriela Mistral was born Lucila Godoy Alcayaga. After working as a teacher until 1930, she started a diplomatic career. Her poetic soul is expressed in melancholy poems that are full of love for God, her native land, humanity and especially children. In *Desolación*, which appeared in 1922, we sense the closeness of death which she experienced when her lover was murdered. In *Poeme de Chile* she describes the country in verse. Gabriela Mistral is the only Latin American woman to have won the Nobel Prize for Literature (in 1945). She died in the USA in 1957.

The poet Vicente Huidobro (1893–1948) was a passionate supporter of Dadaism and is said to have 'created poems in the same way nature creates trees'. He was the founder of the Creacionismo movement, which set the poet the task of creating a new reality. The tradition was continued by Nicanor Parra (born in 1914), the brother of singer Violeta Parra, in his *Antipoemas*, in which he contrasts the poetry of nature with unnatural city life.

During the latter part of the 20th century Chilean novelists gained ascendancy worldwide. Manuel Rojas (1896–1972) won the country's prize for literature for his classic *Hijo de Ladrón (Son of a Thief)*. José Donoso (1924–96) was regarded as Chile's most important contemporary author (despite living in Spain for many years) and his works, such as *Coronation*, explore the boundaries between reality and imagination and the complexities of Chilean society. Isabel Allende (born in 1942 and famous niece of Salvador Allende) gives her books about life in South America a sociopolitical and spiritual dimension; particularly successful is her first work *The House of the Spirits* (1982), which was filmed by Danish director Bille August.

Isabel Allende

On the stage and screen, too, Chile has achieved critical acclaim. The play *Death and the Maiden* by Ariel

Dorfman (born in 1942), about a woman who believes a house guest is her former torturer, became famous after a Broadway production and was also filmed by Roman Polanski in 1994. Antonio Skármeta (born in 1940) is another name to look out for; until 1989 he lived in Berlin, where he wrote various political tales and screenplays.

Recently a new generation of authors has appeared whose work reflects Third World reality, with its social contrasts, and rejects consumer-led society. They include Alberto Fuguet *(Mala Onda)*, Marcela Serrano and the versatile author Luis Sepúlveda (born in 1949), whose novel *Un Viejo que Leía Novelas de Amor (The Old Man Who Read Love Stories)* has been translated into 18 languages.

As far as works on Chile are concerned, one fine novel is Bruce Chatwin's *In Patagonia*, which he wrote in 1974 on a long journey in South America. In brilliant prose he tells the story of the first settlers and their descendants.

Pablo Neruda – poet and collector

The greatest of Chile's poets (1904–73) attracted literary acclaim as early as his schooldays, which was when he decided not to publish under his real name of Ricardo Eliecer Neftalí Reyes but the pseudonym Pablo Neruda. After joining the diplomatic service as a consul at 23, he represented Chile in Burma, Ceylon, Java and Malaysia, and in Spain from 1934 onwards, where the poet Gabriel García Lorca introduced him to the artistic circles in Madrid.

But Neruda felt the urge to return to his native land in 1945 and stayed there as a senator for three years. From 1948 to 1952, during the presidency of Gabriel González Videla, he lived in exile in Europe, receiving the Lenin Peace Prize in Moscow. Meanwhile, he married the Chilean Matilde Urrutia, to whom he dedicated his book *100 Love Poems*. In 1970 he was appointed ambassador in Paris by Chile's socialist president Salvador Allende, and it was there in 1971 that he heard he had been awarded the Nobel Prize for Literature. In the eulogy it said: 'Neruda has been awarded the prize because he creates a poetry that is so elemental and powerful that it gives life to the future and to the dreams of a continent.' His poetic language is an expression of his limitless imagination and immense emotionality. His most renowned works include *General Song, Elementary Odes, Residence on Earth* and *Memories of Isla Negra*.

The poet's travels abroad also inspired him to collect all kinds of things, including ships' figureheads, pictures, paintings, crockery and stuffed animals. These he kept in his three houses: La Chascona in Santiago, La Sebastiana in Valparaíso and Isla Negra near El Tabo. In 1973 Neruda returned to Chile, and died there during the same year, shortly after the military coup on September 11.

83

Pablo Neruda

Food and Drink

Although Chilean cuisine has strong indigenous roots, European influence is evident everywhere. Spain gets the lion's share, of course, while the influence of the 19th-century German settlers is clear farther south.

The country's different climatic zones guarantee an opulent selection of fruit and vegetables all year. In summer, the roads are lined with stalls offering the pick of the season: plums, peaches, apricots, cherries, melons, strawberries, blackberries, kiwis and, as autumn approaches, the famous Chilean grape, sweet and luscious. And, during the winter, there are *chirimoyas* (custard apples), a sweet and fragrant fruit grown mostly around La Serena, which is best eaten with a dressing of orange juice.

Centolla – *delicacy from Patagonia*

The several thousand kilometers of coastline and numerous inland lakes provide a wealth of seafood, including *congrio* (kingklip), a gourmet favorite, *corvina* (sea bass), *merluza* (hake) and *albacora* (swordfish). Farmed salmon, for which Chile is famous, is also ubiquitous.

Many regard the *centolla*, or king crab, which lives off the coasts of Patagonia, as the greatest seafood delicacy there is. It is cooked like lobster, then served either cold with mayonnaise or grilled in a cheesy sauce. A Chilean Sauvignon blanc is just the thing to wash it down.

85

In the rural areas, everyone is particularly delighted if they are invited to an *asado al palo*, where a cow, sheep or suckling pig is slowly roasted over a spit. People are greeted with a *pisco sour* – a very strong grape spirit with lemon and sugar, possibly made a little milder with egg-white. The sauces at these roasting occasions include *pebre*, made from *ají* (chilli pepper), garlic and fresh coriander *(cilantro)*, or *chancho en piedra*, made from peeled tomato pieces, onions, garlic, fresh coriander and parsley. The spicy food is usually accompanied by an excellent *vino tinto* from the well-known estates of the Valle Central *(see pages 57–8)* or with *chicha* – a fermented grape juice whose alcoholic effects are usually noticed far too late.

In the far south, around the Magellan Strait, *cordero* (lamb) is more common than beef. Grazing on the area's virtually virgin pastures, dampened by sea winds, it is reputed to have a special taste and goes mostly to export markets rather than other parts of Chile.

Curanto

One typically Chilean dish is the stew *cazuela*. Chicken or beef is fried briefly, then simmered with onion, garlic, potatoes, maize, beans, peas, carrots, pumpkin and rice, and finally garnished with parsley.

Empanadas are frequently served on public holidays. These pastry turnovers are filled with a mixture of chopped beef, olives, raisins, hard-boiled eggs and onions, or sometimes cheese, and then fried or baked.

Smoked clams from Puerto Montt

Pastel de choclo is another popular specialty. A meat mixture similar to the one for *empanadas* is covered with a maize paste, then baked in the oven and sprinkled with sugar. *Humitas* are another variant with clear indigenous origins: a maize paste with onions, milk and spices is prepared, then wrapped in maize leaves and boiled.

Around Puerto Montt, on Chiloé and in Patagonia, one very popular festive dish is *curanto*. Layers of seafood, chicken pieces, mutton, pork, potatoes and sausage are placed one above the other, and the whole thing is covered with the thick leaves of the *nalca*, a form of giant rhubarb, and cooked for an hour. Traditionally a hole is made in the ground and hot stones are placed inside it, but more often the dish is cooked in vast pots above a gas flame, when it is called *pulmay*.

In central Chile, *huesillos con mote* are often served at the roadside, and are a very popular dessert at simple rural meals. *Huesillos* are dried yellow peaches, and *mote* wholewheat ears. The latter are cooked with ash in water until they lose their husks and turn yellow, then put out to dry. The two are eaten together cold.

If you are invited to tea, there may be *alfajores* on the table, round wafers made of flour, egg yolks and a dash of *pisco*. The very thin rolled discs of dough are baked in the oven and then joined by a layer of *manjar*, a cream made of milk and sugar which gains a thick consistency by being simmered for two hours.

Restaurant selection

Here are some restaurant suggestions for some of the places featured in this guide. They comprise three categories: $$$ (expensive), $$ (moderate), and $ (cheap).

Antofagasta
El Arrayán, Díaz Gana 1314, tel: (55) 247563. Mediterranean food. $$
Casa Vecchia, O'Higgins 1456. Fine food. $$
Marina Club, Avenida Ejército 0909. Good seafood. $$
Terminal Pesquero, northern wharf of the old port off Aníbal Pinto. Excellent fish and shellfish; lunch only. $

Arica
Maracuyá, Com San Martín 0321, tel: (58) 227600. An elegant place with a terrace by the sea, offering very good international cuisine. $$$
Los Aleros del 21, corner of 21 de Mayo/Baquedano, tel: (58) 254641 Serves typical Chilean cuisine. $$

Calama
Hotel Lican Antai, Ramírez 1937, tel: (55) 341621. Good food in a central location. $$$

Chillán
Centro Español, Arauco 555, tel: (42) 216212. Traditional Chilean-Spanish dishes. $$
Restaurante los Adobes, Parque O'Higgins. Typical Chilean cuisine. $$

Iquique
Centro Español, Plaza A Prat 584, tel: (57) 423284. Try the *pisco sour* made with *limones de pica*. $$$

Pucón
La Marmita de Pericles, Fresia 300, tel: (45) 442431. Alpine food in cozy candlelit setting. $$$
Hostería École, General Urrutia 592, tel: (45) 441675. Excellent vegetarian food. $

Santiago
Akarana, Reyes Lavalle 3310, tel: (02) 231 9667. Imaginative food in pleasant surroundings. $$
Café Torres, Avenida Bernardo O'Higgins 1570, tel: (02) 688 0751. Typical Chilean cuisine. $$

San Pedro de Atacama
La Estaka, Caracoles 259, tel: (55) 851201. Tacky decoration, but excellent food. $$

Temuco
La Estancia, R Ortega 02340, tel: (45) 220287. Serves good meat dishes. $$
Club Alemán, Senador Estebanez 772, tel: (45) 240034. Offers both German and international cuisine. $$

Valdivia
Café Haussmann, B O'Higgins 394, tel: (63) 213878. *Cruditos* (marinated raw beef) and German cakes. $$
Cervecería Kunstmann, Camino a Niebla Km. 5, tel: (63) 292969. Hearty German food. $$

Valparaíso
Bote Salvavidas, Muelle Prat, tel: (32) 251477. Seafood specialties on the waterfront. $$$
Le Filou de Montpellier, Almirante Montt 382, tel: (32) 224663. Excellent French food on Cerro Alegre. $

Villarrica
Tabor, Epulef 1187, tel: (45) 411901. Excellent in every respect. $$

Viña del Mar
Cap Dudal, Avenida Marina 51, tel: (32) 626655. Hotel restaurant in stunning seafront location. $$$

Time for a grill

Enjoying the Patagonian wilderness

Active Pursuits

Rafting and canoeing

There are several really exciting areas for rafting and canoeing in the canals and fjords of Patagonia where, particularly, the Futaleufú River is a white-water paradise. The rivers are categorized from one to six, with six the most dangerous. Adequately scary runs from four to six include the Maipo River near Santiago; the Tinguiririca near San Fernando (south of Rancagua); the uppermost reaches of the Río Claro with its impressive Radal Siete Tazas waterfall; or the Río Bío Bío – the lower rapids have been destroyed by a hydroelectric dam – which is for experts only. With the snow-covered Callaqui volcano in the distance, this trip takes you through forest, rocky ravines and mountainous landscapes.

Riding

Follow in the hoofbeats of the *Libertadores* San Martín and O'Higgins, and cross the Andes on a seven-day trek – or take a short morning trot. Contact The Club Ecuestre La Reina, Talinay 11040, Santiago, tel: 02 273 1136.

In the forests of Patagonia

Trekking

How about a six-day tour of the grand Cordillera del Paine in Patagonia? Or why not soak up the remoteness of The Great North by having a relaxing bathe in the geysers of 4,300m (14,100ft)-high El Tatio? Skiing regions (*see opposite*) are also good for hiking in the summer.

Mountain biking

You can follow the trail of the Incas through the desert, or ride up to the icy glaciers *(ventisqueros)* of Patagonia. Bicycles can be rented at most resorts. If you feel like biking in Patagonia in January or February, there's a good Tur del Sur from Puerto Montt to Tierra del Fuego. The 2,000km (1,200 miles) are divided into four sections, each eight to 10 days. Contact Pared Sur in Santiago, Juan Esteban Montero 5497, tel: 02 207 3525, fax: 02 207 3160.

Mountain climbing

Andinismo is the general term in South America for all activities related to mountain climbing in the High Andes. More information is available from: Federación de Andinismo de Chile, Almirante Simpson 77, Santiago, tel: 02 222 0888; Club Andino Osorno, O'Higgins 1073, Osorno, tel: 64 2 32297; Latitud 90, Avenida Kennedy 7268, tel. 02 247 9100; and Altue Active Travel, Encomenderos 83, 2nd Floor, Santiago, tel: 02 232 1103.

Skiing

Skiing down the slopes of still-smoking volcanoes is quite an experience. The skiing season is from June to September, and there are superb skiing areas all over the country. Just 50km (30 miles) from Santiago, at 2,300m (7,545ft), Farellones, La Parva and Valle Nevado have excellent slopes. The pistes of Portillo extend almost as far as the border with Argentina, and can be reached in two hours by car from the capital (164km/87 miles). In the south of Chile, the Termas de Chillán is also a very popular center. More information about resorts is available on www.skicentral.com or www.chileanski.com.

A country made for skiing

Water sports

Many spots along the coast of Chile are becoming internationally popular for surfing. In addition, Chile's lakes are ideal for water sports, including sailing, waterskiing and windsurfing. Equipment can be rented in clubs or from special firms. Since the mountains are so close, katabatic (downhill) winds often blow across the lakes in the afternoons, so it's best to be careful.

Lago Villarrica

Fishing

There is plenty of fishing on Chile's many lakes and rivers, although there are restrictions on seasons and the amount you can catch. And, in some remoter spots, you may even be able to catch a *corvina* (sea bass) from the beach and, certainly, dig some *almejas* (clams) or *cholgas* (mussels) out of the wet sand. More recently, the south of Chile and, particularly, Patagonia has become a prized international destination for fly-fishing. Lodges are located in beautiful, remote spots and provide a luxury service, but the prices are steep. Contact the tourist information office in Santiago for details *(see page 94)*.

Getting There

By air

Around 40 airlines from all over the world fly regularly to Santiago. From Europe, there are over 20 direct flights a week, mainly from Madrid, Frankfurt and Paris, with a flying time of around 15 hours, while six non-stop flights each day connect the United States to Chile, leaving from Miami, Atlanta, Dallas, New York and Los Angeles. In addition, there are four direct flights a week from New Zealand, with a connection from Australia.

When you arrive in Santiago's Aeropuerto Internacional Arturo Merino Benítez, there are buses, minicabs and taxis to drive you the 26km (15 miles) into the city center.

If you intend to make a tour of the South American countries, flights with Chile's main national operator LAN are available from Peru, Bolivia and Argentina to regional airports in the north of Chile but, in most cases, international flights go only to Santiago. Air travel within South America is generally expensive, so it is usually cheapest to buy flights from Chile's neighbors as part of a package from an international tour operator. While in Chile, if booking LAN flights to neighboring countries or within the country, don't hesitate to use the company's electronic booking service (www.lanchile.com); it is very efficient and the ticket really will be waiting for you at the airport.

All national and international flights have to be confirmed 72 hours before departure – a phone call suffices. On international flights, be prepared to pay airport tax of US$26 unless this has already been included in your ticket.

By land

Most travelers arrive in Chile by air as travel overland from its border countries can be unreliable and is extremely slow, hot and crowded. Some of the crossings, especially from Argentina, are also subject to closure with no advance warning due to adverse weather. From Peru the route overland is from Tacna to Arica, serviced by bus and taxi.

From Bolivia, there is a choice of bus or train, though both are slow, packed and uncomfortable. The main bus routes are from La Paz, via Visviri or Tambo Quemado, to Arica; or from La Paz, via Oruro and Colchane, to Iquique. A weekly train service trundles from Oruro to the border village of Ollague, where you cross to the Chilean town of Calama, which has bus connections with Antofagasta on the coast.

Travel overland from Argentina is subject to the weather, as all routes involve crossing the High Andes. The best crossing is from Mendoza or Buenos Aires to Santiago, along Ruta 60 and through the Los Libertadores tunnel. There are also weekly buses from Salta across to Arica, Iquique and Antofagasta.

Opposite: the Valley of the Moon (Valle de la Luna)

91

Calama airport

Long-distance driving

Getting Around

By plane

Chile has two main national airlines: LAN and Sky Airline. There are also smaller companies such as Lassa and DAP that serve specific local routes within the country. although some cheap offers are available, especially for last-minute bookings (visit www.lanchile.com), prices are expensive compared with European flights, but not much more than the sum cost of bus travel and accommodations. If you're planning to fly in January or February, flights may be fully booked.

City bus in Santiago

92

By city bus

Historically, bus travel in Santiago was memorable, with the buses, known as *micros*, racing beside each other in groups of three or four because drivers were paid according to the number of tickets they sold. But a radical modernization of the city's public transport, due to start operation in mid-2005, promises to put order – and more safety – into the chaos.

The city's subway – the *metro* – is slightly more expensive than the buses, but is clean, comfortable and safe, although service stops relatively early at night. There are three lines: one runs east-west beneath Av. B O'Higgins and on through Providencia, while the other two link residential suburbs in the south of the city to this line,

By overland bus

Chile has a dense bus network and travel is cheap. There are four types of bus: simple vehicles that travel short distances; the comfortable Pullman or Clase Turista buses for medium distances (simple meals and TV are included in the price); the Salón Ejecutivo, a luxury-class bus with plenty of leg room and sleeper seats; and the Salón Cama luxury sleeper buses similar to the first-class section of a jet airplane. The last two types include pillows, blankets and a drink in the price, plus TV. Long distances are driven at night.

By cab

Taxis colectivos, or 'collective taxis', stop anywhere along their fixed routes. Individual taxis are cheap and the meter usually functions – but make sure it's been switched on and don't take the taxis that park outside major hotels. Radio cabs are particularly pleasant at night because their drivers can phone you when they reach the front door. Trips at night and weekends are more expensive than in the day and fares are likely to double after 9pm.

Inside Concepción station

By rail

Sadly, rail travel in Chile is a shadow of its past glories. The remaining services cover only destinations between Santiago and Temuco in the the south. There are no services to the north or the coast. Chile's railroads have largely been superseded by buses, but the journey from Calama to Oruro (32 hours) is unforgettable: the train climbs to above 4,000m (13,200ft), and quite a few Indians use it. Trips are once a week. The Santiago–Temuco route (almost 12 hours) is covered by a train that runs every night and booking a berth in the 1920s German sleeping car is worth the supplement. For details on all rail, travel contact: Empresa de Ferrocarriles del Estado, Alameda 3170, Santiago, tel: (02) 585 5000.

Hire car

Car hire is relatively expensive, especially in the provinces. However, in some places, it is well worth the cost, particularly if you share the expenses with other travelers. For example, in the Lake District and the Central Valley, having one's own transport opens up many more opportunities. There are international firms (Avis, Hertz, Budget) as well as national ones. The Automóvil Club de Chile, which has offices all over the country, also rents out cars, and drivers to go with them if required; members of other automobile associations receive discounts. You will be expected to leave a blank credit-card printout, and foreigners require an international driver's license. Make sure you take out comprehensive vehicle insurance.

The open road **93**

Driving

Although traffic in Santiago is hectic, driving outside the city is easy. The north-south Panamerican Highway (Ruta 5) and the main east-west roads of central Chile are safe and modern, with all the facilities you would expect in Europe or North America. The speed limit on these highways is generally 120kmph (75mph) and speed checks are frequent and strict. Alcohol and drugs at the wheel are forbidden, and seatbelts are mandatory.

Santiago has a number of new high-speed roads with an electronic toll system. These roads can be used without the windshield-mounted bleeper but a daily pass, available at most service stations, should be acquired either before or after using the highway.

Serving the south

By cruise ship

Cruises are the ideal way of getting to know the southernmost tip of the continent. Several services run from Punta Arenas to the southern tip of Tierra del Fuego. The best is the luxurious seven-day *Terra Australis* cruise. For details contact: Cruceros Australis, Av. El Bosque Norte 0440 Piso 11, tel: (562) 4423110, www.australis.com.

Negotiating the fjords

Route marker in the north

Facts for the Visitor

Visas and passports

All foreigners, except residents of neighboring countries, require passports to enter Chile, and a few of these must obtain visas, but all tourists from the UK and the USA need is a valid passport. A tourist card is issued to all foreigners on arrival. Visitors from some countries are charged an administration fee (United States, US$100; Canada, US$55; Australia, US$34 and Mexico, US$100), which must be paid in cash. The tourist card contains your identification data and is generally valid for 90 days. It is renewable for a further 90 days.

Keep your copy of the card carefully until you leave; if you do happen to mislay it, a substitute can be obtained from Policía Internacional, Gral. Borgoño 1052, Santiago, or from any regional police station.

Tourist information

Up-to-date material and information can be obtained from the headquarters of the state tourist information office: Senatur, Avenida Providencia 1550, Santiago, tel: 02-731 8331, fax: 2361417. There are also branches in all the big cities.

The Chilean Embassy in London supplies booklets and brochures for visitors to Chile *(see Diplomatic Representation, page 97)*. In the US the Chilean Embassy operates a separate tourist information division at 1732 Massachusetts Avenue NW, Washington DC 20036, tel: 202-530 4108.

Money matters

There is no limit on the amount of foreign currency that can be taken in or out of the country. The Chilean currency unit is the peso (written Ch$), and notes come in denominations of 1,000, 2,000, 5,000 10,000 and

20,000Ch\$, with 5, 10, 50, 100 and 500Ch\$ coins. One US dollar will buy you around 585Ch\$ (as of mid-2005). Foreign currency can be exchanged in all the cities and towns, as well as at larger hotels. You can withdraw money from automated teller machines (ATMs) affiliated to the Plus and Cirrus systems, found everywhere except in the very smallest towns (although not all machines permit operations with overseas bank accounts). Travelers' checks, though safer than cash, may be difficult to exchange in smaller towns. Credit cards are widely accepted in towns.

Electricity
The voltage in Chile is 220V, and adapters for the three-prong plugs are available at the airport, or in hardware stores.

Time
Chile is on US Eastern Standard Time, five hours behind GMT and six hours behind CMT. Daylight Savings Time is from early March to early October.

Telecommunications
Airmail to Europe takes between five and 10 days, and up to three months by ship. Stamps can be purchased at any post office and in most major supermarkets. Faxes can be sent from most hotels and from Entel and CTC offices; and Internet cafés abound even in small towns.

The time in Punta Arenas

Telephone
There are numerous public payphones that can be operated with cash or phonecards. For long-distance calls you have to dial the precode of one of the phone companies and then the country, local code and number; so for calls from an Entel phonebox (the country's largest long distance operator), you dial 123 then 044 for calls to England, or 123-01 for calls to the US.

The code for Chile for incoming calls is 0056, followed by the area code and then the number. The area code for Santiago is 02 and for Concepción 041 (omitting the 0 if you are calling from abroad). All Santiago telephone numbers have seven digits, but elsewhere in the country they have six digits.

Opening times
Banks: Monday to Friday 9am–2pm.
Shops: Monday to Friday 9am–8pm.
Department stores: Monday to Friday 10am–9pm, Saturday to 2pm.
Post offices: Monday to Friday 8am–6pm, Saturday 9am–12.30pm.
Telephone offices: Monday to Friday 10am–10pm.

Holidays and festivals

January 1 New Year's Day

January International classical music festival in Frutillar (Semanas Musicales)

February Song festival in Viña; Muestra Cultural Mapuche, traditional music and dancing of the Mapuches, Lago Vaillarica

March National rodeo championships in Rancagua

April Good Friday, Easter Sunday

May 1 Labor Day

May 21 National holiday commemorating the sea battle at Iquique

June Corpus Christi

June 29 St Peter and St Paul

Festival in San Pedro

July 16 La Tirana (popular pilgrimage festival near Iquique)

August 15 Ascension Day

September 18 *Fiestas Patrias*, popular festivals on Independence Day

September 19 Army Day with parade

October 12 Discovery of America Day *(Día de la Hispanidad)*

November 1 All Saints' Day

December 8 Immaculate Conception

December 25 Christmas

Parading in Valparaíso

December 26 High point of the pilgrimage festival in Andacollo

December 31 Official firework displays, in Santiago and – the largest one in the country – Valparaíso.

What to bring

Chile is probably the most materially modern country in South America, with exhaustive shopping potential in Santiago, so if you forget to pack something, you'll probably be able to purchase it there. Because of the extreme differences in temperature it's advisable to have a woolen jacket with you even in the warmer zones, and always carry some kind of wind and rain protection when down in the south.

Earthquakes

Rule number one – don't panic.

In buildings: take cover under doorframes or sturdy furniture such as tables, and try to keep as far away as possible from windows or glass doors; on no account use elevators.

In built-up areas: do not walk out in the street because of the danger of falling buildings.

In the open: do not stay close to buildings, trees or electric cables.

On country roads: avoid bridges or any elevated sections of highway.

Photography

Film is only slightly more expensive than in Europe or the US. Please ask Indians for permission before photographing them, and respect their right of refusal.

Health precautions

Vaccinations are not required. Anyone planning to spend time at high altitudes should ask their physician for advice before leaving for their vacation, however. It's better not to drink water straight from the tap – especially in the warm north.

Medical treatment

Medical standards in Chile are high. Doctors *(médicos)*, public emergency services *(Asistencia Publjca or Posta de Urgencia)* and private clinics can be found all over the country. If you need assistance in one of these, you will have to prove your credit-worthiness with a card or cash. UK visitors should take out medical insurance so they can recoup any costs.

Pharmacies *(farmacia)* sell most medication by international manufacturers; all-night branches are listed in the daily newspaper *El Mercurio*.

Dental treatment in Chile is also of a high standard. Ask at your hotel for a recommendation.

Life jackets are essential at the San Rafael glacier

Emergencies

Police: 133
Police information: 139
Fire department: 132
Accident: 131

Crime

Chile has one of Latin America's lowest crime rates, particularly as regards violent crimes, and you can travel through the country without danger. Just take basic precautions: watch out for pickpockets in crowded places and in large cities, avoid out-of-the-way areas at night. At night a woman on her own is safer calling for a radio taxi, rather than flagging a cab down in the street.

Diplomatic representation

UK: 12 Devonshire Street, London W1G 7DS, tel: (020) 5580 6392
US: 1736 Massachusetts Avenue NW, Washington DC 20036, tel: (202) 785 1746.

Gratuities

In restaurants service is not generally included and a 10 percent tip is usual. Taxi drivers do not expect to be tipped, but it's usual not to ask for any small change owed to you.

Hotel Termas de Puyuhuapi

Accommodations

Chile provides everything from international luxury hotels in Santiago to family-run boarding houses in the country. In the cities, *aparthotels* – serviced apartments – are popular. Hotels and clubs have sprung up in the resorts along the coast, providing inexhaustible leisure opportunities, along with *cabañas* (hotel complexes with individual holiday houses). *Hosterías* are country hotels, *hostales* simple hotels and *residenciales* boarding houses (usually with a shared bathroom). In small towns and villages you'll find private rooms, or *piezas*. The Chileans are relatively impervious to noise, so do ask about the proximity of a hotel to the street and so on before you book.

Prices not only vary according to classification but also whether the region is considered attractive for tourists. Rooms in *residenciales* cost around US$10 a night, while single rooms in luxury hotels in Santiago can be US$200–350. To foster tourism, overseas visitors are exempt from the 19 percent value-added if they pay in dollars (cash or travelers' checks) or with an overseas credit card. Price differences between single and double rooms are generally less than 10 percent. Chile's tourist office, Senatur, publishes an annual hotel brochure, *Alojamiento*, for each region.

Financially far more attractive, and very popular as a result, are package deals for hotel stays lasting several days, whether you're on your own or in a group. These include sports facilities and a guide if you are in the mountains. The package deal for several days is called *todo incluido*, all-inclusive, and that means everything from the airport transfer to wine with meals.

A useful tip is to visit some of Chile's plentiful thermal

spa resorts, some of which incorporate fantastic hotels with all the spa services you'd ever need. These are just the places to wind down, and are always in magnificent locations: near volcanoes in the south, or on the edges of fjords, such as at Puyuhuapi in Patagonia, where you can hop from a hot spring into a cold ocean with views of the eternal snows.

Youth hostels can be found in the most popular tourist areas. There are around 500 campsites in Chile, sub-divided into supervised and unsupervised sites, and in five categories (ranging from 'no amenities' to 'very comfortable'). Camping in the open is forbidden, especially in reserves.

Hotel selection
Here are suggestions for some of the main centers featured in this guide, listed according to the following categories: $$$ (expensive), $$ (moderate) and $ (inexpensive). Reservations for many of the hotels can also be made on the Internet at www.chile-hotels.com.

Antofagasta
Hotel Antofagasta, Av. Balmaceda 2575, tel: (55) 228811, fax: (55) 268415, www.hotelantofagasta.cl. Large hotel with all modern facilities including pool and excellent view of the port. $$$
Holiday Inn Express, Av. Grecia 1490, tel: (55) 228888, fax: (55) 285457, www.ichotelsgroup.com. Slightly out of the way, but very pleasant. $$$
Hotel Diego De Almagro, Condell 2624, tel: (55) 268331, fax: (55) 251721. A comfortable and centrally located hotel. $$
Rawaye, Sucre 762, tel: (83) 225399. Simple and central. $

Arica
Hotel Arica, Av. Com. San Martín 599, tel: (80) 254540, fax: 231133. Four-star hotel on one of the city's best beaches. $$$
Central, 21 de Mayo 425, tel: (80) 252575. Friendly. $$
Hotel Lynch, Patricio Lynch 589, tel/fax: (80) 231581. Simple, clean and friendly. $

Calama
Park Hotel, Camino Aeropuerto 1392, tel: (55) 319900, fax: (55) 319901. Situated between the airport and city center, there's a pool and very good restaurant. $$$
Hotel El Mirador, Sotomayor 2064, tel: (55) 340329, fax: (55) 340329, www.hotelmirador.cl. Central and comfortable. $$
Residencial Splendid, Ramírez 1960, tel: (55) 341841. Simple but clean. $

Cozy option in Puyuhuapi

Antofagasta Hotel

Castro

Hotel Unicornio Azul, Pedro Montt 228, tel: (65) 632359, fax: (65) 632808. Lovely hotel with a good view over the harbor. **$$$**

Hostal Chilote, Aldunate 456, tel: (65) 635021. Family-run hotel in central location. **$**

Chaitén

Hotel Mi Casa, Avenida Norte, tel/fax: (65) 731285. On a hill, with a good restaurant. **$$**

Hospedaje Lo Watson, Ercilla 580, tel: (65) 731237. Friendly. **$**

Chillán

Gran Hotel Isabel Riquelme, Arauco 600, tel: (42) 213663, fax: (42) 211541. Pleasant hotel on the main square. **$$$**

Hotel Rukalaf, Arauco 740, tel: (42) 230393, fax: (42) 233366, www.rukalaf.cl. Comfortable and very central. **$$**

Claris, 18 de Septiembre 357, tel: (42) 221980. Friendly atmosphere. **$**

Residencial 18, 18 de Septiembre 317, tel. (42) 211102. Good value. **$**

Concepción

Holiday Inn Express, Av. San Andres 38, tel: (41) 489300, www.ichotelsgroup.com. Hotel near the airport. **$$$**

El Araucano, Caupolicán 521, tel: (41) 230606, fax: 230690. Central hotel. **$$$**

Hotel Ritz, Barros Arana 721, tel: (41) 226696. Centrally located. **$$**

Residencial Colo Colo, Colo Colo 743, tel: (41) 227118. Bright rooms. **$**

Copiapó

Hotel Diego de Almeida, Bernardo O'Higgins 656, tel: (52) 212075. Centrally located with a pool. **$$$**

Hostería La Casona, Bernardo O'Higgins 150, tel & fax: (52) 217278. Colonial-style hotel with attractive grounds. **$$**

Palace Hotel, Atacama 741, tel/ fax: (52) 212852. Good value. **$**

Coyhaique

Hostería Coyhaique, Magallanes 131, tel: (67) 231137, fax: (67) 233274. Relatively new guesthouse in a beautiful park setting. **$$$**

Easter Island

Casas Rapa Nui, bookings through Santiago office, tel: (02) 2066060, fax: (02) 2284655. Two lodging houses belonging to the local Explora luxury hotel chain. **$$$**

Hotel Hanga Roa, Hanga Roa, tel/fax: (39) 100299. Comfortable hotel on the bay with a pool. **$$$**

Frutillar
Hotel Salzburg, Camino Playa Maqui, at northern end of the bay, tel: (65) 421589, 421599. Big rooms in well-appointed wooden bungalows. **$$$**
Hotel Klein Salzburg, Av. Philippi 663, tel: (65) 421201 or 421599. Central, with a superb view. **$$$**
Hotel Ayacará, Avenida Philippi 1215, tel: (65) 421201, www.hotelayacara.cl. Charming colonial-style establishment. **$$**
Kaisersee-Haus, Avenida Philippi 1333, tel: (65) 421387. By the water, with large rooms. **$**

Iquique
Arturo Prat, Aníbal Pinto 695, tel: (57) 427000, fax: (57) 429088. Central four-star hotel. **$$$**
Hostería Terrado Suites, Los Rieles 126, tel/fax: (57) 488000. Situated by the Cavancha Beach. **$$$**
Hotel Barros Arana, Barros Arana 1302, tel: (57) 412840, fax: (57) 426709. Comfortable place on the edge of the center. **$$**
Residencial Baquedano, Baquedano 1315, tel: (57) 422990. Centrally located. **$**

Isla Robinson Crusoe
Hostería Alcalde Daniel Defoe, tel: (2) 751075. Cabins in the town of San Juan Bautista. **$$**
Residencial Mirador Selkirk, Pasaje del Castillo, San Juan Bautista, tel: (32) 751028. Lodging in a family home. **$**

Osorno
Gran Hotel Osorno, O'Higgins 615, tel: (64) 232171. Situated on the main square, with 70 rooms. **$$**
Hotel Rayantú, Patricio Lynch 1462, tel: (64) 238114, fax: (64) 238116. A modern hotel five blocks from the main square. **$$**
Residencial Schulz, Freire 530, tel: (64) 237211. **$**

Portillo
Hotel Portillo, tel/fax: (02) 3617000. Swish resort hotel with all-inclusive skiing packages. **$$$**

Pucón
Hotel Antumalal, Carretera Villarrica 23, tel: (45) 441011, fax: (45) 441013, www.antumalal.com. Small luxury hotel beautifully located by a lake. **$$$**
Gran Hotel Pucón, C Holzapfel 190, tel: (45) 442112, www.granhotelpucon.cl. Renovated beach mansion. **$$$** .
La Tetera, Urrutia 580, tel/fax: (45) 441462, www.tetera.cl. Guesthouse run by Swiss/Chilean couple. **$$**

Kids in Puerto Montt

San Pedro vernacular

Puerto Montt
Hotel Viento del Sur , Ejército 200, tel: (65) 258701, fax: (65) 314732. Located on a hill, and tastefully furnished. **$$$**
Residencial Urmeneta, Urmeneta 290, tel/fax: (65) 253262. One of the better cheap choices in a city that's poor on hotels. **$$**

Puerto Natales
Hotel Costaustralis, Pedro Montt 262, tel: (61) 412000, fax: (61) 411881. Luxury hotel on the waterfront. **$$$**
Hotel Juan Ladrilleros, Pedro Montt 161, tel: (61) 415978. Friendly service with good views. **$$$**
Concepto Indigo, Ladrillero 105, tel/fax: (61) 413609, www.conceptoindigo.com Small, fun hotel with vegetarian restaurant. **$$**

Puerto Varas
Hotel Colonos del Sur, Del Salvador 24, tel: (65) 233369, fax: (65) 233394, www.colonosdelsur.cl. Well-equipped modern hotel facing lake, with pool. **$$$**
Casa Azul, Manzanal 66, tel: (65) 232904, www.casaazul.net. Quaint and comfortable hostel. A few private baths. **$–$$**

Punta Arenas
Hotel Cabo de Hornos, Plaza M Gamero 1025, tel: (61) 242134, fax: (61) 229473. Old and elegant hotel. **$$$**
Hotel José Nogueira, Bories 959, tel: (61) 248840, fax: (61) 248832, www.hotelnogueira.com. A *palacio* converted into an elegant hotel. **$$$**
Hostal O'Higgins, O'Higgins 1205, tel/fax: (61) 227999. Rooms with/without bathroom. **$–$$**

Puyuhuapi
Hotel Termas de Puyuhuapi, tel: (67) 325103. A great place to splash out but very difficult to get into except as part of a package deal. **$$$**
Hostería Alemana, Otto Uebel 450, tel: (67) 325118. Clean and attractive. Helpful owner. **$**

San Pedro de Atacama
Hotel Explora, bookings through Santiago office, tel: (02) 2066060. Luxury hotel offering all-inclusive deals. **$$$**
Hostería/Camping Takha-Takha, Caracoles 101, tel: (55) 851038. Quaint cabins and serviced camping ground. **$**

Santiago
Hyatt Regency, Av. Kennedy 4601, Las Condes, tel: (02) 2181234, www.hyatt.com. International-style luxury. **$$$**
Hotel Plaza San Francisco (Kempinski), Av. B O'Higgins 816, tel: (2) 639 3832, fax: 639 7826. One of the few good hotels in the downtown area. **$$$**